BREAK ▼ POINT
BUSINESS PROCESS REDESIGN

The Coopers & Lybrand Performance Solutions Series

David K. Carr
Kevin S. Dougherty
Henry J. Johansson
Robert A. King
David E. Moran

Carr, David K., Dougherty, Kevin S., Johansson, Henry J., King, Robert A.,
and Moran, David E.

BreakPoint Business Process Redesign

Library of Congress Catalog Number 92-054916
ISBN 0-944533-04-3

Other Books by
Coopers & Lybrand

Excellence in Government:
Total Quality Management in the 1990s
(1991)

Process Improvement:
A Guide for Teams
(1993)

Measuring Quality:
Linking Process Improvement to
Customer Satisfaction
(1993)

TABLE OF CONTENTS

Page

Acknowledgements   i
Introduction   iii
How To Use This Book   ix

SECTION 1

Business Breakthroughs for the 1990s   1
Chapter 1
Breakthrough! Leaping Ahead of the Competition   3
Chapter 2
Making Dramatic Change Happen   23
Chapter 3
BreakPoint BPR: Changing the Way
     America Does Business   41

SECTION 2

Making BPR Work: Essential Factors for Success   51
Chapter 4
Assessing Customers, Competitors, and Capabilities   53
Chapter 5
Getting the Right People Involved   65
Chapter 6
Information Technology:
     Creating Advantage or Paving Cow Paths?   87
Chapter 7
Change Management   101

Chapter 8
    BPR and Continuous Improvement:
      Choose Both, Use Both   123

SECTION 3

    BreakPoint BPR: Beyond Process Improvement   141
Chapter 9
    Creating Breakthroughs   145
    Phase I: Discover   147
    Phase II: Redesign   166
    Phase III: Realize   175
Chapter 10
    What It Takes To Be a Breakthrough Organization   181
Appendix A
    Bibliography   191
Appendix B
    BPR Glossary of Terms   195
Appendix C
    About the Authors   199

ACKNOWLEDGEMENTS

One of the great difficulties of writing about a new approach to management is that its best practitioners usually are deeply engaged in the effort, and have little time or interest in pausing to tell their stories. Also, many consider (and rightly so) that how they made their breakthroughs has the same value as a trade secret. This is particularly true when the subject is business process redesign (BPR), with its urgent sense of action and fast, high pay-off in competitive advantage.

Thus, we express our sincere appreciation to key clients whose breakthrough experiences and results are the guiding force of this book:

Allied-Signal Corporation

AT&T

Bank of Boston

Dun & Bradstreet

Jacksonville, Florida, Naval Aviation Depot

Medrad

Norfolk, Virginia, Naval Public Works Center

PHH FleetAmerica (a division of PHH Corporation)

Although the literature on BPR is as yet fairly sparse, we have reviewed that which is available and incorporated some of the authors' findings and comments in this book, including those of Robert Foster of Coopers & Lybrand. Appendix A references these works.

The Coopers & Lybrand's management consulting team who gave us the benefit of their insights and experience include partners Grady Means, Ian Littman, Alex Beavers, Mike Blum, Les Shindelman, Helen Ojha, Andrew Molenaar, Larry Mendenhall, Hank Cooper, Bill Smillie, and Fred Viskovich, and staff members Beth Raymond, Patty Adam, Mike Bear, Cliff Cooksey, Debra Eshelman, Maryann Gately, Spencer Haddock, Karen Vander Linde, Craig Monroe, and Ken Williams. Last, but not least, we wish to acknowledge the superb research, editorial, and administrative work of project manager Steven Clyburn, Joy Mara, and Mary Anne Reilly, and the contributions of Lynne Morton, Mary Ann Fitzgerald, and Diana Borruso of Coopers & Lybrand's National Office.

INTRODUCTION

Thomas Edison wasn't out to make a better candle when he invented the light bulb. He first demonstrated this breakthrough invention by lighting up, literally and figuratively, an area of lower Manhattan called Wall Street—and launched whole new industries.

This book is also about lighting up Wall Street, Capitol Hill, the eyes of your customers, or any other place or people that can make or break your future. But instead of inventions, our focus is on *breakthroughs in process performance*. These processes—the way work is done—create, make, sell, and distribute products and services. It is about creating world-class processes like those of Edison's "invention factory." The first modern R&D laboratory, it was capable of turning out a new product every day and a breakthrough like the phonograph once a week.

Why this focus? Because at the close of the most inventive century in human history, inventions are not America's problem. *Processes* are our problem.

For example, Americans invented television and video cassette recorders, but today few in this country are employed by the companies that make these products. Instead, we have become the world's largest retail outlet for other countries' automobiles, consumer electronics, clothing, toys, and a host of other products.

Because of their antiquated, inefficient processes, many of our best companies are losing (and in some cases have already lost) the global race to produce better products and services faster, with higher quality, and at lower cost. Most government agencies are making this situation even worse. Every day they shorten the fuse on the budget deficit time bomb, yet still cannot shore up the nation's crumbling physical and human infrastructure.

Organizations (and countries) that are falling behind cannot afford to wait around for gradual improvement; doing things five or ten percent better than before just won't cut the mustard. Instead, they need to switch on the afterburners and blast past the competition—they must have process breakthroughs. But these breakthroughs won't happen unless industry and government take radical steps to change how they do their work. That's what *business process redesign* is all about.

Business Process Redesign

Business process redesign (BPR) is one term used to describe how organizations achieve radical improvement over a short period. Other names include business redesign, process redesign, and business re-engineering. The operative word in BPR is "redesign": to change a business process from stem to stern so that it delivers the strongest possible competitive advantage.

Such redesign is not a casual or easy undertaking. It requires vision, willpower, and a comprehensive approach to change that includes these elements:

- Leadership and guidance from top management throughout the effort;

- An external orientation in seeking why and how to improve processes, based on customer research, competitive and economic analysis, and benchmarking;

- Top level strategy to guide change, and leaders who can implement change;

- Sound methods for redesigning work processes to meet strategic performance goals;

- The use of advanced information technology to enable breakthrough performance;

- Effective change management to adjust an organization's people and culture to new ways of working; and

- Continuous improvement methods to sustain and increase the dramatic gains achieved during break-throughs.

Coopers & Lybrand has helped many organizations in business and government to use these elements in comprehensive planning that leads to world-class results. The experience of our clients and our professionals can be found in BreakPoint BPR, our approach to business process redesign.

BreakPoint BPR

BreakPoint BPR shares many of the characteristics of business and process re-engineering. These characteristics include viewing a business process not in terms of the artificial structure of departments, divisions, or functions, but rather as a single, integrated flow of work. Also, we see process redesign and information systems re-engineering as concurrent efforts, instead of one preceding the other.

But there are key differences. First, BreakPoint BPR is a growth strategy, not simply a means to downsize or cut costs. It focuses on creating strategic-level competitive advantage through breakthroughs in the *core business processes that most affect customers and shareholders*. This focus is embodied in what we call the breakpoint: a strategic target level of performance that creates market response far in excess of the resources required to achieve it.

Yes, the methods of BreakPoint BPR can be applied to less important processes to reduce costs and increase their performance. It is very effective at doing this, as you will see in the chapters to come. But give more attention to the examples we provide on breakthroughs in core business processes—these are the ones that really count. Those process breakthroughs did more than win a race: they left competitors choking in the dust.

The second difference is that we view employees and managers, not redesigned processes or technology, as the chief source of competitive advantage. For this reason, BreakPoint BPR aims at helping your people adopt the new types of *behaviors, values, and culture* needed to make breakthrough processes operate at peak performance: customer focus, teamwork, open communication, risk-taking, and sound decision-making.

Finally, BreakPoint BPR is about *change leadership*, the role executives must fervently embrace to make breakthroughs happen. In today's turbulent economic environment, the only constant is change, and the only way to help your organization change is to lead it. This is why this book is not simply a technical treatise on the mechanics of BPR, which can be delegated to managers and specialists. Rather, it is a guide for executives, the leaders of change.

About Coopers & Lybrand

Coopers & Lybrand, founded in 1898, is one of the world's oldest and largest accounting and management consulting firms. Throughout the world, Coopers & Lybrand has more than 64,000 partners and professional staff working in 112 countries. In the U.S., we have 16,000 professional staff located in 101 cities.

Over the years, our many clients have asked us to assist them in developing management and information technology solutions for improving their businesses. This led us to create a Management Consulting Service (MCS) that now includes over 2,000 professionals in the United States and 3,000 overseas. Clients who use our BPR services include:

- Fortune 500 companies engaged in manufacturing, transportation, communication, retail, and financial services;

- Health care providers ranging from major hospitals to health maintenance organizations;

- Federal government organizations in both the civilian and defense sectors; and

- Institutions of higher learning, including major universities.

In this book, these clients will tell you in their own words why they decided to go for breakthroughs, how they put together the right teams for radical change, the obstacles they encountered, and the major successes they achieved.

Our Responsibility to You

As the authors of one of the first (if not the first) book on business process redesign and re-engineering, we have certain responsibilities to you, the reader. The first is to provide the basic principles and mechanics of BPR as we, our clients, and others see them. Second, we are required to prove these principles and methods by showing detailed examples of how they have been applied in real life. By doing this, we hope you will come away with sufficient information to make decisions as to if, how, and when BPR will be useful in your organization.

Also, BPR is new and not completely defined. Many will claim to use it when they are simply rebundling their same tired management methods in shiny new packages. Thus, we feel a responsibility to you and our profession of management consulting to set, through this book, standards for judging all approaches to process redesign and re-engineering.

David K. Carr
Kevin S. Dougherty
Henry J. Johansson
Robert A. King
David E. Moran

Coopers & Lybrand
October 1992

HOW TO USE THIS BOOK

For your convenience, we divided this book into three sections which cover, respectively, the background, principles, and methods of business process redesign (BPR), with emphasis on BreakPoint BPR. To accommodate the busy reader, each section is preceded by a quick listing of its main points, as is every chapter in the section. Short summaries follow each chapter.

The three sections are:

Section 1, *BreakPoint BPR: Breakthroughs for the 1990s*, is an overview of process breakthroughs (Chapter 1), business process redesign (Chapter 2), and Coopers & Lybrand's BreakPoint BPR approach (Chapter 3). This section provides a context for the rest of the book, and includes dozens of examples of breakthrough results.

Section 2, *Making BPR Work: Essential Factors for Success*, discusses five essential elements of our approach to BPR: assessing customers, competitors, and an organization's capabilities (Chapter 4), choosing the right people to work on BPR projects (Chapter 5), using information technology and process redesign together (Chapter 6), managing the human and organizational factors of major change (Chapter 7), and using BPR and continuous improvement as a combined strategy for long-term competitive advantage (Chapter 8).

Section 3, *BreakPoint BPR: Beyond Process Improvement*, details the two important aspects of our approach. In Chapter 9, we show the three-phase approach our clients favor:

- *Discover,* which includes setting performance targets, assessing current performance, and creating high-level plans for redesign;

- *Redesign,* which is the detailed planning of process,

organizational, information system, and human
changes; and

- **_Realize,_** which covers the implementation of the
planned changes.

Chapter 10 outlines seven characteristics of an organization
capable of making and sustaining breakthroughs in business
process performance—a necessary core competency for future
prosperity.

Appendix A is a bibliography, Appendix B is a glossary of
terms, and Appendix C provides background information on the
authors.

Business Breakthroughs for the 1990s

◆

After two decades of falling behind in global competition, many American companies need a breakthrough to put them back out in front—or to survive. While a 10 percent improvement used to mean success, beating the competition today may require 50 percent to 100 percent improvement, or even more.

◆

A new approach to creating customer-focused radical change, business process redesign (BPR), is helping many companies achieve the competitive breakthroughs they need.

◆

Successful BPR challenges the status quo throughout the organization. The results? A new vision of what a company can be and new ways of doing business that create long-term competitive advantage.

CHAPTER 1

BREAKTHROUGH! LEAPING AHEAD OF THE COMPETITION

CHAPTER HIGHLIGHTS

◆

How breakthroughs put companies out in front:
three case examples.

◆

Self-assessment: does your company need a breakthrough?

◆

Why breakthrough is becoming the theme of the 1990s:
corporate need, new opportunities, new
technological/methodological capabilities.

Business Breakthroughs:
Success Stories for the '90s

The Bank of Boston: Winning with Flexibility

In the late 1980s, a new chief financial officer, Peter Manning, joined the Bank of Boston (BOB). He soon realized that the bank had a much greater profit potential than it was currently showing. For example, the bank's ancillary financial services provided minor revenues, while competitors prospered because they offered better value on key measures such as cost-per-account and cost-per-transfer.

At BOB, ancillary financial services is a $25 million transaction business that involves "backroom" operations such as handling stock transfers, dividend and interest payments, and pension plan administration. Revenues are measured as tiny percentages of the face value of financial documents. Thus, profits depend on efficiency and productivity. Quality and security must be absolute—mistakes can cost customers millions of dollars.

To determine why competitors were outperforming them in this line of business, Manning and a team of senior executives led an examination of BOB back room processes. They found that BOB provided financial services through six different groups in 11 locations. Work for one customer could move through many different systems, for example, one for dividends, one for transferring stock ownership, and one for bond interest. Each separate operation added costs. Coordination was a major problem, and quality was difficult to monitor and control.

Many of these service operations were simply huge rooms with row upon row of grey metal desks, where workers used long-outmoded procedures that resembled old-style factory assembly lines. Stacks and boxes of financial documents formed the aisles of these old facilities, and customers who

4

toured them were, to say the least, not confident of the bank's efficiency, quality, or security.

With a goal of offering the lowest-cost, highest-quality financial services in their market, the Bank of Boston needed a breakthrough. Working with Coopers & Lybrand, they found it in a technique used in manufacturing: the flexible factory, in which people, machines, and processes can be quickly reconfigured to handle different products or demands. This was exactly the dynamism needed in modern financial markets, which introduce new products almost daily.

Collapsing the six groups into one, the bank trimmed staff size and relocated most group activities to one new building in suburban Canton, Massachusetts. While the more centralized operation produced valuable cost savings, the innovative design of the new office space has been the key factor in attracting new customers and dramatically increasing market share.

Features such as modular "plug-in" work stations that can be reconfigured overnight give customers visual proof of operational efficiency. Such flexibility means that a new handling process can be quickly designed to meet the requirements of any financial document. A streamlined system for handling documents and modern information technology ensures against bottlenecks in processes—which created the stacks and boxes of paper in the old environment.

"Our work systems and staffing approach complement the flexibility of our physical design," notes John Towers, who heads the new securities department. "For example, in the old days if we gave new work to a manager, he or she might say, 'Sure, but give me 20 or 30 more people for the job,' and go about business as usual. Under the new system, in a few hours our managers can lay out a streamlined, efficient process for handling each new account without needing dozens of additional staff.

"From what customers and others tell us, no one in our market can respond more quickly to new service requirements or surges in workload than we can. Today we do 80 percent more securities processing business with 17 percent fewer employees."

The Farm Journal:
Exploiting New Technology by Redesigning Processes

In the early 1980s the trade magazine *Farm Journal* faced bankruptcy because it could offer advertisers only a general, undifferentiated audience for print ads. Further, as the number of farmers in America declined, so did the *Journal*'s base rate for these ads. Smaller, more specialized magazines and direct mail had given advertisers a cheaper way of targeting farms with certain characteristics (i.e., type of crop or cattle, equipment and chemicals used, size of farm, etc.).

In 1984, the *Journal* completely redesigned its process for "building" a magazine using a new technology called selective binding, and now produces up to 5,000 customized versions of a single edition, a plus for readers and advertisers alike. Each version provides articles and advertising that match the individual characteristics of 800,000 farms across the country. This breakthrough spurred the *Journal* out of its financial crisis into a 1991 valuation of $250 million.

This initial breakthrough led to others. Today, the *Journal* gets added revenues from its extensive farm data base by conducting market research studies for farm product makers. This new competency opened up another business opportunity; agribusiness giants like John Deere, Pfizer, and Ciba-Geigy now contract with *Farm Journal* to maintain *their* proprietary data bases on sales and distribution.

Allied-Signal/Bendix: Opening New Markets by Reducing Cycle Time and Cost

Bendix Automotive Services is a major producer of anti-lock brakes, a product whose expense had limited its market to large or luxury vehicles. Customer research showed, however, that cutting the cost and weight of anti-lock brakes in half while maintaining safety standards would increase the market for them by 500 to 1000 percent. They would also have to reduce time-to-market to beat the competition and meet customer demand.

To meet the challenge, Bendix worked with Coopers & Lybrand to make radical changes in its product development process for anti-lock brakes by:

- Redesigning the product development process to feature concurrent, rather than sequential, activities; streamlined process steps; and new enabling tools such as bookshelving for product families, using parametric design concepts, and a new information architecture.

- Instituting cross-functional innovation teams for advanced product development.

- Developing and implementing a global manufacturing plan that minimized the need for capital investment.

- Using product cost modeling to assist in meeting cost reduction goals.

"These innovations enabled Bendix to exceed its objectives," says Alex Beavers, managing partner of Coopers & Lybrand's Center for Operations Technology in Burlington, MA. The new product design required 70 percent fewer parts, cost less to produce, and cut production time by 50 percent. Time-to-market fell from five years to two-and-a-half years. Costs fell by 60 percent for an estimated savings potential of tens of millions of dollars. Best of all, the new process produced a range of advanced, higher quality products centered around the consumer."

Why Many American Businesses Need Breakthroughs Now

Today, we have the techniques and the technology to create stunning, dramatic advances in competitive power like those in the preceding examples. The growing list of success stories is inspiring many companies to move away from a slow and steady short yardage offense. By rewriting the playbook, these visionary businesses are dazzling customers, shareholders, and the competition with moves they've never seen before.

Does your company need a breakthrough? In assessing their own companies on the criteria in the box on the following page, many of today's executives would have to answer "Yes." Let's discuss why.

It is no secret that the global competitive environment has changed radically, placing new demands on American competitors. Yet the functional approach to business processes ingrained in many companies has compromised their ability to respond to the new realities. Despite major improvement efforts, gaps have widened instead of closed. Because many businesses no longer satisfy their customers, competitors have appropriated those customers.

As a result, many American businesses that used to be world leaders now need breakthroughs just to survive. Others need breakthroughs to give them the momentum they need to close the competitive gap and take their shot at market dominance.

Competing Today: New Players, New Rules

Twenty years ago, American businesses dominated world markets in products from semiconductors to tractors. Yet in a comparison of two ten-year periods, the lists of world industry leaders looked very different, according to international business expert C.K. Prahalad's study of selected industries. The following chart from his study shows how successful foreign businesses were in challenging America's giants.

8

Does Your Company Need A Breakthrough?

If any of the following questions describe your situation, your company may need radical, breakthrough changes in its business processes.

1. New product development is critical to your success, but your competitors are getting their products to market months and even years faster than you are.

2. You are employing many more people to do a job than your chief competitors do. Don't think about your industry's average—you have to benchmark against the guys who someday just might eat your lunch.

3. You need to cut costs significantly and quickly because competitors are offering the same products at lower prices than you are.

4. You want to improve productivity by more than 50 percent within the next two years.

5. Customers are demanding faster delivery or processing, and you don't know how to speed up the job.

6. You can't meet your customers' fundamental needs for product and service quality at an affordable cost.

7. Your company's market share is substantially less than it used to be or than you want it to be.

8. You want to go global—take your products and services overseas or tie into an international trade network.

9. Government regulation or environmental concerns dictate that you find a new way of doing business.

10. You have tried other ways of improving your situation [e.g., downsizing, productivity initiatives, total quality management (TQM), automation] and they haven't produced the competitive leap forward you want and need.

11. Market changes or shareholder dissatisfaction threaten your company's survival.

12. You are planning to introduce a major new information system, or re-engineer an existing system, that you hope will provide competitive advantage.

Industry	Leaders in 1970-75	Leaders in 1980-85
Automotive	Ford and GM	Toyota, Nissan, Honda, Ford, GM
Tire	Goodyear, Firestone	Goodyear, Michelin, Bridgestone
Semiconductor	Texas Instruments, Motorola	NEC, Toshiba, Fujitsu, Hitachi
Financial Services	Bank of America, Chase, Citicorp	Nomura, many others
Tractors	Caterpillar	Komatsu

Prahalad and others explain the newcomers' success as a function of the changing nature of competition itself. Yesterday's basis of competition has become today's price of admission to the market, and new dimensions of competition now influence market success, as shown in Figures 1-1 and 1-2.

- **New product innovation.** Providing good quality and low prices is no longer enough. Customers expect these conditions but increasingly are asking for high-quality new products, as well. An ability to innovate has helped Japanese companies such as Canon, Honda, and NEC to grow between 250 percent and 350 percent in an eight-year period. This new product-based growth (as opposed to acquisition-based growth) is matched by few U.S. industries.

FIGURE 1-1

RELENTLESS FORCES OF CHANGE
CONTINUE TO PRESSURE
NORTH AMERICAN ENTERPRISES

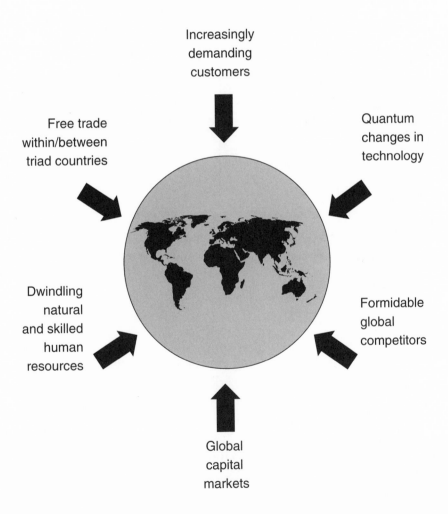

FIGURE 1-2

THE BASIS FOR COMPETITION
CONTINUES TO SHIFT

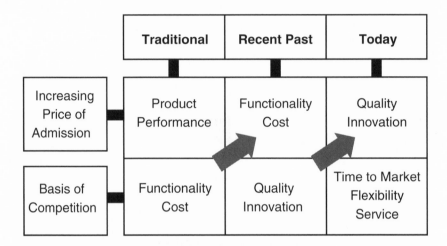

	Traditional	Recent Past	Today
Increasing Price of Admission	Product Performance	Functionality Cost	Quality Innovation
Basis of Competition	Functionality Cost	Quality Innovation	Time to Market Flexibility Service

Yesterday's basis of competition has become today's price of admission and new dimensions of competition have been introduced.

- **Time-based competition.** Many of today's successful companies are killing the competition with speed. Decreasing time-to-market and providing faster customer service with no loss in quality have given many companies a competitive advantage. For example, after the Raychem Corporation reduced its manufacturing lead time from 100 to three days, it tripled its business over the next three years.

- **Competency-based competition.** Increasingly, companies are competing not only on the basis of end products and services but on the basis of the core competencies they possess.

For example, 10 years ago, Wal-Mart stormed the discount retailing industry by developing a new competency in distribution and transportation. Its system involves continuously delivering goods to Wal-Mart's warehouses for selection, repacking, and delivery to stores. Products move from loading dock to loading dock in 48 hours or less, which gives Wal-Mart two types of savings to pass on to customers: price reductions from ordering full truckloads of products and additional economies from avoiding inventory and handling. In addition, the variety of goods Wal-Mart can make consistently available also leaves the competition far behind.

"We stock over 80,000 items in our stores, and our warehouses directly replenish almost 85 percent of their inventory, compared to only about 50 percent or 65 percent for our competition," said Wal-Mart's founder, the late Sam Walton, in his autobiography, *Sam Walton: Made in America.* "As a result, the gap from the time our in-store merchants place their computer orders until they receive replenishment averages only about two days. That probably compares to five or more days for a lot of our competitors, which don't ship as much merchandise through their own network.

"The time savings and flexibility are great, but the cost savings alone would make the investment worthwhile. Our costs run less than 3 percent to ship goods to our stores, while it probably costs our competitors between 4.5 to 5 percent to get those same goods to their stores. The math is pretty simple: if we both sell the same goods for the same price at retail, we'll earn 2.5 percent more profit than they will right there."

To achieve a competency competitors haven't been able to match, Wal-Mart made strategic investments in support systems, such as a private satellite communications network that sends point-of-sale data to 4,000 vendors and a transportation system serviced by about 2,000 company-owned trucks.

"Distribution and transportation have been so successful at Wal-Mart because senior management views that part of the company as a competitive advantage, not as some afterthought or necessary evil," explained Joe Hardin, executive vice president for logistics and personnel at Wal-Mart. "A lot of companies don't want to spend any money on distribution unless they have to. Ours spends because we continually demonstrate that it lowers our costs."

Work Processes: Boxed into Business as Usual

A few years ago, General Motors (GM) spent about $30 to $40 billion to automate its processes. This approach failed to produce the desired return because the functionally aligned processes themselves needed massive change to meet the challenge of foreign competition.

The track record of one highly automated GM plant provides a case in point. After making a reputed $650 million investment in high-tech automated systems, this Michigan plant took, on average, nearly 34 hours to build cars that each had an average of 1.37 defects. By comparison, a nearly 40 percent less automated NUMMI (New United Motors Manufacturing Incorporated, a GM/Toyota joint venture in Fremont, California) plant spent 19 hours producing cars that averaged 0.69 defects—**nearly half** the number of those manufactured in the Michigan GM plant.

Worse yet, automation at GM became a barrier to improvement by further entrenching outdated processes and making them less flexible. While GM took eight years to design and produce the Saturn, for example, Japanese competitors launch new product lines about every three years. Chrysler recently achieved this goal with its LH models, again through radical process redesign along with automation.

Total quality management (TQM)–style improvements have helped American organizations streamline many unwieldy, small-scale processes. However, the big picture—the complete, cross-functional processes that stretch from order to delivery to collection—has received less attention because of the functional specialization traditional in American management. In the absence of a trans-functional perspective, many of today's most important business processes are fragmented, building in major barriers to performance. For example, Daniel Whitney tells the story of a household appliance manufacturer whose compartmentalized product design process drove the company out of business. They literally could not build an important new product because of functional log jams such as these:

- Product designers insisted on a shape and style that could not be manufactured to provide the close tolerances product engineering required.

- The assembly process built only complete products for testing, not modules. If a product didn't work when tested, the whole appliance had to be taken apart to find out why.

- A functional management organization meant that managers had neither an overall perspective on the problem nor the authority needed to solve it.

As a result of functional paralysis, many businesses now need massive cross-functional process breakthroughs to produce the efficiencies and capabilities that lead to market success.

"Many companies must completely revamp their functional approach to processes and find the competency that's hidden in those linear boxes," says Len Olin, the Coopers & Lybrand partner who helped AT&T redesign outdated processes and enhance competitive potential. "Nothing short of radical change can help you reduce order-to-delivery times from a month to a day or cut multi-year product development cycles by 50 percent."

Robert Foster, a managing associate in Coopers &

Lybrand's financial services practice, points out another reason some industries may need immediate, massive process improvements: government regulation. "In the New England area, government regulatory demands for information are forcing banks to think about changing their systems and processes radically. Without breakthrough changes that allow automatic retrieval of the required information, for example, the banks must mount a labor-intensive secondary process whose only value is achieving regulatory compliance."

A Big Gap Needs a Big Leap

A large corporation recently asked Coopers & Lybrand to assess its productivity program. To remove a 30 percent cost disadvantage, the company had taken a variety of traditional improvement approaches:

- Appointing a corporate productivity manager;
- Establishing productivity committees;
- Increasing industrial engineering staff by 50 percent;
- Carrying out operation-by-operation analyses to improve efficiency;
- Retraining employees to work "smarter, not harder;"
- Streamlining work flow and material movement;
- Replacing out-of-date equipment;
- Retooling operations to cut operator time;
- Tightening standards;
- Emphasizing good housekeeping and cleanliness; and
- Installing a computer-based, measured-day work plan that allowed daily performance reports.

After all this effort, productivity had risen only seven percent. Profits remained negligible, and the company's market share continued to fall.

While our analysts found many specific problems with the program, five main issues doomed this functionally oriented approach to limited success:

- Improvements in one area were offset by declines in others. When improvement initiatives are functionally focused, they can't take critical interrelationships into account.

- Improvements occurred in processes that didn't have a major impact in meeting goals. For example, improvement efforts were not focused on value-creating processes and customer or shareholder needs.

- The focus of efforts was internal, not external.

- Programs were oriented toward middle managers, not toward the senior executives who can address problems broader in scope.

- Short-term improvements were not sustained.

This example is typical of the limited ability of functionally oriented improvement efforts to effect major change. Nor do efforts to improve competitiveness based on size have breakthrough impact. For instance, in the automotive, aerospace, and banking industries, acquisitions have exhausted the competitive advantage of being large in scale. Many in these industries have played out earlier restructuring paths and need a new competitive edge to move ahead.

The opposite approach, downsizing, often leaves substantial untapped potential for competitive advantage. While estimates suggest that about one-third of American companies have downsized every year for the past three years:

- More than half of the 1,468 restructured companies surveyed by the Society for Human Resources Management had the same or a lower level of productivity after implementation.

- A poll by Right Associates found that 74 percent of senior managers at recently downsized companies said that their workers had low morale, distrusted management, and feared future cutbacks.

- A review of recently downsized companies shows that rather than leading to a healthier, more competitive company, downsizing most often leads to more downsizing.

The reason downsizing alone does not produce breakthrough results is simple. Cutting staff without changing work objectives, work processes, or corporate structure merely leaves fewer people to do the same jobs.

Factors such as these underline the need for American businesses with world-class aspirations—or threatened survival—to look at the potential of breakthroughs for their companies. While radical change may be unsettling, nothing short of that may get results. Paul O'Neill, the president of ALCOA, explained his company's rationale for leaping forward rather than taking a slow and steady, incremental approach to change:

"Continuous improvement is exactly the right idea if you are the world leader in everything you do. It is a terrible idea if you are lagging in the world leadership benchmark. It is probably a disastrous idea if you are far behind the world standard. In too many cases we fall in the second and third categories. In these cases, we need rapid, quantum-leap improvement. We cannot be satisfied to lay out a plan that will move us toward the existing world standard over some protracted period of time— say 1995 or the year 2000—because if we accept such a plan, we will never be the world leader."

Leaping Ahead of the Competition:
Today, We've Got What it Takes

The 101st Congress of the United States introduced no fewer than 611 bills addressing the need to improve the competitiveness of American businesses. The sole purpose of one bill was to commit America to "plan to remain the strongest and most competitive nation on earth."

While economic supremacy is part of our national self-image, it takes more than an act of Congress to make it a reality. Today a new methodology, described in Chapter 2, gives us the ability to make the breakthroughs that can renew our competitive advantage. Called business process redesign (BPR), this radical new approach integrates and enlarges the scope of existing business improvement disciplines and applies them simultaneously to the corporate-wide processes that make or break performance. This "hit 'em with everything we've got" approach is one reason why dramatic changes, such as those in the examples below, can occur so rapidly today. Another reason is that 1990s information technology creates new ways of doing business that would not have been possible even 10 years ago.

Business process redesign is an evolving discipline that only began to take shape in the late 1980s. Its full potential to help American businesses leap ahead of the competition has not begun to be realized. Yet it is already much more than a theory. The list of companies whose situations have improved after using BPR techniques is long and growing. A few additional examples from Coopers & Lybrand's experience show why the new breakthrough methodology is producing so much excitement.

- A few years ago, a $100 million electronic power supply manufacturing company serving the telecommunications and computer markets, was losing out to competitors because its product costs were high and its time-to-market slow. Using BPR techniques, they reduced their cost of assembly and their cycle time by 80 percent each.

- An electronics firm wanted to be an OEM (original equipment manufacturer) supplier, but several aspects of its operation were holding it back: cycle time was too long, costs were too high, yield and capacity were too low. They used BPR to reduce lead time by 80 percent, reduce costs by 30 percent, and increase capacity by 600 (yes, 600) percent.

- A strategic business unit of a Fortune 50 company reassessed its marketplace and core competencies as part of BPR. The new vision translated to $150 million in savings over three years.

- A British firm cut back the number of its factories from three to two, generated extra capacity, and saved one million British pounds. These changes required comprehensive business process redesign, which produced an additional four million pounds in savings.

- A high-tech company used BPR techniques to reduce lead times by 95 percent. They also reduced work-in-progress levels by 75 percent.

Results like these show that BPR is creating business breakthroughs today. Companies now have the potential to change as much as necessary to surpass the competition and increase value for customers and shareholders.

Summary

- New global competitive realities are prompting American businesses to rethink the traditional functional approach to business processes. Many corporations are finding that they need breakthroughs to achieve or maintain market dominance; others require breakthroughs in order to survive.

- Former corporate leaders are learning that producing quality products at comparatively low prices no longer guarantees success. Process-oriented approaches, such as new product innovation, time-based competition, and competency-based competition are putting former second-tier performers ahead of the pack.

- Functionally oriented approaches to improving corporate productivity, acquisition-based strategies to increase corporate profits, and traditional downsizing efforts all have one thing in common: They have a limited capacity to effect major change. Breakthroughs are often necessary to maintain or achieve a competitive edge.

- BPR, a new methodology, integrates and broadens the scope of current business improvement approaches and applies them to critical corporate-wide processes. A vast array of American companies have discovered that BPR works.

CHAPTER 2

MAKING DRAMATIC CHANGE HAPPEN

CHAPTER HIGHLIGHTS

◆

How Connecticut Mutual Life Insurance Company
took days off its policy-change process and improved
customer satisfaction and the bottom line.

◆

How BPR integrates and flows
from the industrial quality improvement tradition.

◆

Key principles of BPR: what it does and
why it's more effective in
producing dramatic results.

Connecticut Mutual:
Better Customer Service for a Better
Bottom Line

Not too long ago, when Connecticut Mutual Life Insurance Company customers wanted to name a new beneficiary to their policies, the process took days. Someone would take the information by phone and fill out a handwritten form, then pass it down the line. Next, a clerk pulled a paper copy of the policy from a file, filled out another handwritten form, and sent it to be word processed. After a check for errors (and there were often errors), the form was redone, a copy put in the file, and another mailed to the policy-holder. With too many steps that created extra paperwork, this old-fashioned approach to processing changes wasn't efficient. It was no longer acceptable in the eyes of customers—-in today's business climate, they expect instant response.

Today, the process has been redesigned. Now phone repre-sentatives use computer work stations to make all the needed changes while the policyholder is on the phone—a matter of min-utes. A confirmation of the transaction goes out to the policy-holder in hours. No delays, no chance for a document to get lost, fewer errors, and a 13 percent reduction in staff. More important, this responsive service at the customer "front-line" provides immediate, visible value that promotes customer loyalty.

Connecticut Mutual invested $5 million in redesigning its process to exploit the efficiencies of imaging and other tech-nologies that are the key to its breakthrough. Originally, the com-pany estimated a two-year time to pay back this cost. But the project broke even four months early, and the savings came from more than just the technology. Now, one supervisor can work with 20 or 30 people, which helps the company move toward a more horizontal organizational structure—the corporate shape of the future.

The Breakthrough-Maker:
Business Process Redesign

Over the past decade, management specialists have realized that urgent competitive challenges and tougher customer demands such as those faced by Connecticut Mutual, require companies to move further and faster than traditional improvement approaches alone could take them. Like Connecticut Mutual, they need dramatic reductions in cycle time and cost, improved productivity and quality, and changes that impress customers and improve the capacity to compete. As noted in Chapter 1, techniques such as cycle time reduction, total quality management (TQM), and the introduction of new technology have been and continue to be the "price of admission" to competition and the foundation of excellence. Yet while they are necessary, they have not been sufficient to produce the magnitude of change—or the speed of change—that companies facing severe competitive pressures often desperately require.

To respond to that need, management specialists worldwide have tested and refined a new methodology that links and emerges from these traditional industrial improvement approaches. Called business process redesign (BPR) or re-engineering, this new methodology achieves fast, breakthrough change by enlarging the scale of improvement. Instead of applying improvement techniques to individual functions and isolated processes that may not be central to a company's success, BPR works at a company-wide level. To focus the improvement effort for maximum results, it identifies and works on only the broad, cross-functional processes that lead to competitive advantage.

In Coopers & Lybrand's BreakPoint BPR methodology (described in detail in Section 3), the most potent redesign innovations are based on the company's competitive "breakpoint": the strategic competitive advantage a company can obtain in cost, quality, cycle time, or service that has enough customer

FIGURE 2-1

BPR: THE BREAKTHROUGH MAKER

Continuous Incremental Improvement Provides Small, Ongoing Change	Business Process Redesign Creates Rapid, Revolutionary Change
■ Current Processes Are Reasonably Close to Customer Requirements	■ Existing Processes Are Broken Down or Outmoded
■ Accepts the Status Quo as the Basis for Improvement	■ Challenges the Fundamentals
■ Uses Technology Incrementally	■ Views Technology as a Process Transformer
■ Less Risk Because Impact Usually Is Narrow	■ More Risk Because Impact Is Large, Cross-Cutting
■ Cost of Making Change Usually Is Small, Often "Free"	■ Often Very Large Cost to Make Change

and shareholder appeal to shift the market in its favor. Once these critical targets are identified, many types of improvement methods work interactively to achieve them, using a fast-track timeline and technological support to speed change.

Key Principles of BPR: Revolutionize, but Target Change

To catalyze dramatic change, BPR takes a bold look at

FIGURE 2-2

BREAKPOINT BPR

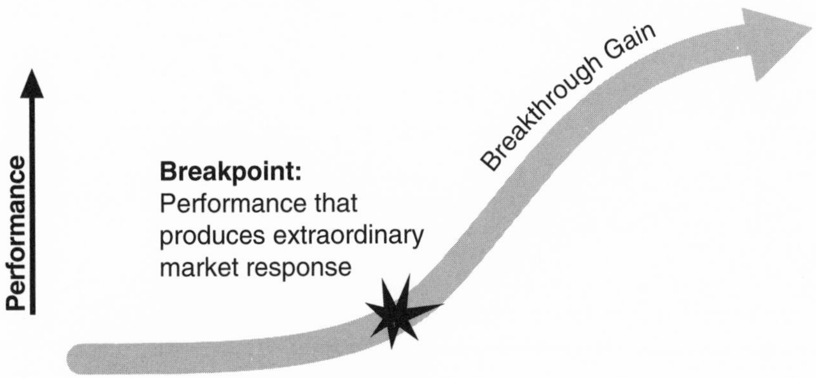

Breakpoint:
Performance that
produces extraordinary
market response

Breakthrough Gain

Performance

what can be, unlimited by the status quo. "We call this 'green-fielding,' because your perspective can be completely fresh, almost as if you were building an operation from scratch," notes Coopers & Lybrand partner Andrew Molenaar, who helped Australia's Qantas Airways regain competitive strength after the 1990 Gulf War drastically reduced airline business. "Qantas had anticipated an increase of 57,000 bookings over the previous year in the February-March, 1990, period; as a result of the Gulf War's dampening effect on international air travel, it got an increase of only 2,000, and losses for the year were up $200 million.

"Our charge was to explore 'all avenues for profit improve-ment.' We worked with their managers to develop plans for rad-ical change in all aspects of the operation, from integrating business processes and restructuring the organization to out-sourcing key functions, selling subsidiaries, and developing a totally new information flow. Overall, we considered changing almost everything but the kangaroo on the tail of the plane, and it worked. Their willingness to envision an innovative approach produced $200 million in savings."

By eliminating sacred cows and "we've always done it that way" thinking, BreakPoint BPR can produce what some call a paradigm shift: a whole new way of looking at your business. For example, Burger King made a paradigm shift when they realized that they are not just in the fast food business; they are also in the real estate business. In a similar way, a cruise line concluded that developing a worldwide reservations system for travel agents would boost their competitiveness more than cruise-oriented changes that passengers would see.

In pursuing innovation and paradigm shift, BPR has five key principles:

- Starting and ending with the customer in envisioning and implementing change.

- Redesigning core business processes (e.g., new product design, order fulfillment from acceptance to delivery, customer service, and field support logistics) because these are the building blocks of operational capabilities, which translate into value and set businesses apart in the minds of customers and shareholders.

- Challenging the fundamental framework in which an organization conducts business.

- Setting ambitious, measurable goals.

- Providing rapid payback.

Starting and Ending with the Customer

Gary Gulden and Douglas Ewers studied a company improvement team that worked diligently to pare expenses from its field services operation and improve the speed with which it answered service calls. Although the team proposed ideas that could have saved the company $50 million, a more fundamental issue emerged: customers resented spending time dealing with service representatives. By looking at the need to change from the customer's point of view, they developed a radically different approach to providing service: storing the products customers needed at the customer's site and providing a toll-free number for customers who needed to request additional products or repairs. This approach saved $100 million, while adding value that customers appreciated.

A customer orientation, which derives from the TQM philosophy, is equally fundamental to successful BreakPoint BPR. Yet the new methodology has broadened the customer focus to include the competitors with whom customers could choose to do business. Harold Sirkin and George Stalk tell the story of a paper mill facing bankruptcy that knew its competitors did not have the machines to produce lower weight/lower cost paper their customers could use. By offering a product line no one else had, they were able to raise their price per ton while still reducing the customer's overall paper costs. They moved from fifth place in their competitive arena to first in two-and-a-half years. Figure 2-3 synopsizes customer criteria that can point the way to similar competitive leaps.

Redesigning Core Business Processes

Traditional improvement initiatives are often process-oriented, but they tend to define the scope of a process narrowly, in a linear, functional way, like that shown in the left half of Figure 2-4. BreakPoint BPR departs radically from traditional thinking, identifying "core" processes that cut vertically across functional, geographic, business unit and even company borderlines, such as that shown in the right half of Figure 2-4. Each core process is initiated by a customer, shareholder, or market need and ends when that need is satisfied. Examples of core business processes include:

FIGURE 2-3

CUSTOMER "VALUE" CRITERIA

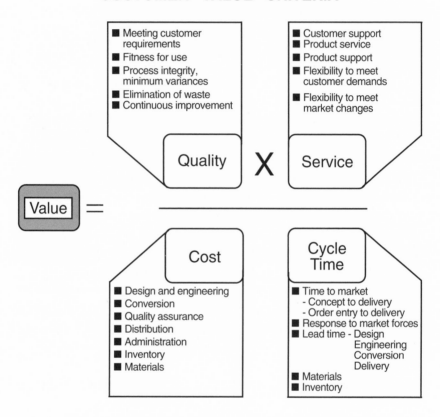

- Order to delivery to cash.

- Need/desire for a product innovation to product design and development to marketing to purchase.

- Service requisition to service delivery to receipt of payment.

Leslie Wexner, president of The Limited, alluded to this "end-to-end" work process concept when he told his employees

FIGURE 2-4

BPR: A NEW PROCESS FOCUS

Competitive advantage is realized by managing customer-oriented processes. . . not linear functions

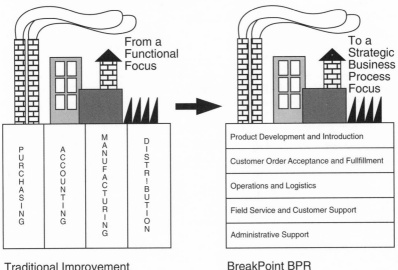

From a
Functional
Focus

To a
Strategic
Business
Process
Focus

P U R C H A S I N G	A C C O U N T I N G	M A N U F A C T U R I N G	D I S T R I B U T I O N

Product Development and Introduction

Customer Order Acceptance and Fullfillment

Operations and Logistics

Field Service and Customer Support

Administrative Support

Traditional Improvement
Methodologies

BreakPoint BPR

that none of their jobs are finished until the cash comes in the door.

While core business processes will differ from company to company, they all have one thing in common: they are the inherent basis of a company's competitive position and, effectively redesigned, can produce new competitive distinctions. Figure 2-5 outlines the kinds of changes BPR makes to maximize the competitive potential of core business processes.

Although BPR usually focuses on a few core business processes for competitive advantage, a parallel need may also exist to redesign crucial support processes, such as financial operations or contracts management, whose poor performance could

FIGURE 2-5

BUSINESS PROCESS
REDESIGN INCLUDES:

Business Process Improvement	Business Design Change	Structural Change
• Eliminate Redundant Tasks	• Realign Overall Process-Flow to Customer Needs	• Align Tasks to Responsibilities
• Minimize Non-Value-Added Tasks or Task-Time	• Realign Process to Value-Chain	• Align Measurements to Responsibilities
• Reduce Work Fragmentation	• Integrate New Product/Service Attributes	• Align Process Flow to Assure Quality at the Source
• Eliminate Bottlenecks to Flow	• Establish New Value-Adding Functions	• Re-Synchronize Training, Methods, and Procedures and System Change Releases
• Balance Demand/Resource Load	• Align Value-Adding Processes to Customer Willingness-To-Pay	• Establish High-Performance Work Teams
	• Redesign Flow for Process, Work Culture, Resource Demand, Customer Need, Value-Adding Fundamentals	• Align Job Types With Processing Paths
		• Align Tasks Scope/Resource Skill to Work Domains and Objects

32

compromise the effects of innovations. In these cases, BreakPoint BPR's aim is to align support performance with the requirements of core business processes.

Challenging the Fundamental Organizational Framework

In addition to challenging process configurations and boundaries, BreakPoint BPR looks at how a company's organization chart, strategy, style, value system, management systems, and job descriptions (see Figure 2-6) can contribute to its competitive strength.

While Connecticut Mutual Life Insurance Company redesigned a core business process to compete more successfully, other companies have found a leading edge in other aspects of their enterprise. C.K. Prahalad's research on smaller companies that have successfully challenged global leaders (e.g., Canon versus Xerox, Apple versus IBM) found that each of them had a culture that was obsessed with winning. This obsession permeated the organization from top to bottom and was nurtured and sustained over the long term. In another case, new management processes were an important advantage for a major international computer vendor because they improved management's ability to make decisions quickly and effectively. The key to success is looking at all aspects of the operation, because companies may find their competitive edge where they least expect it.

Setting Ambitious, Measurable Goals

Tom Peters says that the old aphorism "what gets measured is what gets done" has never been so powerful a truth. This is particularly so in BPR, which uses ambitious goals to establish the required scope of change.

Setting quantifiable objectives is also a fundamental tenet of traditional process improvement. Without concrete goals you don't know where you're starting, and you don't know for sure when you've arrived. BPR differs by pumping up the volume.

FIGURE 2-6

BPR CHALLENGES THE FUNDAMENTAL FRAMEWORK IN WHICH AN ORGANIZATION CONDUCTS BUSINESS

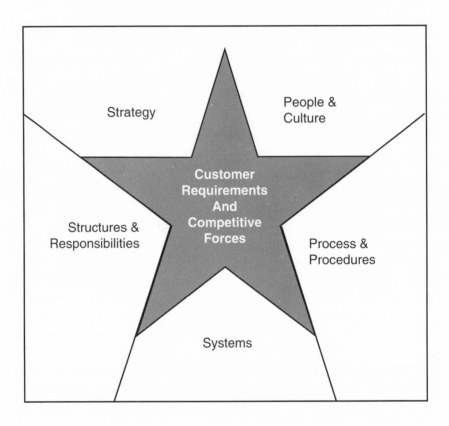

Strategy

People & Culture

Customer Requirements And Competitive Forces

Structures & Responsibilities

Process & Procedures

Systems

FIGURE 2-7

BPR SETS AND MEETS
AMBITIOUS GOALS

Improvement Area	Typical Client Reduction	Household and Personal Care Products Client Reduction
OE/Ship Leadtime	-85%	-80%
Inventory		
• Raw Materials	-70%	-40%
• Finished Goods	-70%	-55%
Changeover Time	-75%	-90/70%
Space Reduction	-50%	-60%
Cost of Quality	-45%	-90/75/65%

Where a continuous improvement initiative might aim for a 25 percent improvement over several years, BPR will start with 60 percent, 80 percent, or even 100 percent improvement targets within two years or less. Figure 2-7 synthesizes several companies' recent experiences.

"As a corollary to Tom Peters' statement, we've found that what you aim for is what you get," notes Coopers & Lybrand's Mike Bear. "If your goals aren't ambitious enough, you won't change enough to produce a breakthrough."

The Xerox Reprographics Manufacturing Group's experience is a good example. During the 1980s, the company began a productivity improvement program to counter a recent drop in its market share. The program produced an eight percent improvement over several years. When then-president Charles

Christ saw a competitor's ad in the *New York Times,* he realized his program had not aimed high enough. The competitor was selling a product similar to a Xerox copier at retail for less than it still cost Xerox to manufacture.

Providing Rapid Payback

To a business that needs a competitive giant step now, a slow breakthrough isn't much of an option. A recent Conference Board survey shows that, with BPR, companies don't have to wait for the magnitude of payback they need. About 55 percent of respondents said that BPR had given results within 18 months; 72 percent began seeing changes within six months of start-up. In all but one case the *annual* financial benefit of BPR was greater than or comparable to the *one-time* cost of redesign.

While BPR requires the supports and perspectives discussed above and in Chapters 4–8 to succeed, it can provide something many would not have believed possible: a long-term quick fix.

All BPR Is Not Created Equal

While this chapter has presented general characteristics of process redesign efforts, it is important to emphasize that BPR efforts can be conducted at strategic or sub-strategic levels, with different project goals.

- **Process improvement.** Some BPR efforts redesign large core business processes simply to improve their efficiency and effectiveness. These productivity-style improvements may be critical to a company's survival, but they are largely driven by internal factors and perspectives, such as correcting recognized process problems or meeting budget objectives. They are not at a strategic level.

- **Achieving parity with competitors.** These BPR projects derive from external factors and perspectives.

Companies use benchmarking to find out why they've fallen behind their competitors. They may conduct research to find out what customers want and use BPR to help them close the competitive gap.

● **Going for the breakpoint.** Coopers & Lybrand's BreakPoint BPR includes these two perspectives, but it moves companies a critical step beyond them. Operating at a high strategic level, BreakPoint BPR looks for the breakthroughs that can create market dominance.

Each of these options is a viable choice that can produce valuable results. However, breakpoint-level BPR has the most dramatic potential. For example, Coopers & Lybrand recently helped a large credit card company plan a BPR program designed to reduce the time it takes for credit approval from its current average of 12 days and extreme of 45 days. Ultimately, research and creative modeling came up with a BPR improvement strategy at each of the three above-listed levels of intensity:

Level 1: Improving the process.

This approach, using no new technology, would institute batch processing of credit and fraud checks and the use of JIT cells to reduce cycle time to 4 or 5 days (a pilot project achieved this goal).

Level 2: Matching other industry leaders.

By using a new client-server technology, featuring direct CPU-to-CPU communication, projections showed the company could trim processing time to a few days. Ultimately, the technology and process changes might allow processing to be completed within 24 hours of application receipt.

Level 3: Creating a breakpoint.

BPR could create a new process that allowed one person to

conduct a credit check via data bases instantly, while the customer waited. Large-scale telemarketing to exploit the potential of "instant approval" could provide a substantial new competitive advantage.

Final decisions have not yet been made, and it is possible that this client will choose all three options, phasing from one to the other as resources permit. While each approach has benefits, only by creating a breakpoint can a company get a breakthrough competitive edge.

Summary

- The most potent BPR innovations are based on a company's competitive "breakpoint": the strategic competitive advantage it must achieve in cost, quality, cycle time, or service to attract enough customer and shareholder support to vault it ahead of its competition. Not all BPR efforts operate at this high strategic level, however, and lower-level projects can still provide valuable results.

- BPR, like its philosophical partner, TQM, is customer/market-driven and results-oriented.

- Everything is a candidate for innovation under BPR: the organization structure, business processes, job responsibilities, and company values. A successful redesign may require realigning all of these areas and more.

- The major focus of BPR is the core business processes that begin with a customer or shareholder need and end when that need is satisfied. These broad horizontal processes create customer and shareholder value and are the basis for a company's competitive capability.

- Like TQM, BPR requires those involved in the

redesign to quantify their objectives. But unlike traditional process improvement, BPR aims for 60, 80, or 100 percent improvements in process performance. What's more, a recent Conference Board survey found that 55 percent of its respondents had seen substantial results within 18 months of initiating BPR efforts.

CHAPTER 3

BREAKPOINT BPR: CHANGING THE WAY AMERICA DOES BUSINESS

CHAPTER HIGHLIGHTS

◆

What redesign looks like:
the paradigm shift at a major insurance company.

◆

Common changes after BPR:
new ways of working with customers and suppliers, new ways
of using information systems, and newly empowered workers.

◆

Organizational values also change
after BreakPoint BPR.

What Redesign Looks Like

" " T alk about a paradigm change," recalls a former senior executive in a major insurance company. "We moved from a system dictated by a division of labor to a process dependent on integration of information—in 18 months. One person and a part-time assistant began doing the jobs of 19 people, with no supervisors checking or double-checking the outcome."

The company's old "underwriting and issue" process began when field agents sent new policy paperwork to a field office, which checked and reworked it and sent it on to the home office for additional processing and underwriting. Under the new approach, the agent works directly with a "case manager," who does more than three-fourths of the related tasks; 10 percent of the tasks are performed by a grey collar worker and another 10 percent by "gold collar" experts in medicine or insurance law. An expert information system completes most of the underwriting tasks, with an interactive feature that allows the system to make recommendations that the case manager can accept, review, or question.

According to this executive, however, another technological innovation was even more important: using the personal computer (PC) as a "worker bee."

"For only a fraction of the cost of the expert system, we put together a program that let the PC do almost all the routine tasks associated with this process. As soon as a case manager began a case, for example, the system would run ahead and check the agent's license and issue the commission. The system was also a tool for reminding the case manager what had to be done next, an important feature in a multi-step task. The system became the reliable personal assistant everyone would love to have."

With the new system in place, the company was a much

different place to work. Instead of a few hundred workers in this process, about 25 percent of whom were "prima donna" underwriters, several dozen people were doing the job on an equal footing. A process that used to take weeks to complete was accomplished in one-fourth of the time or less. While some of the case managers actually missed having day-to-day super-vision, quality soared without it. Checking for errors and rework were no longer part of anyone's job description.

Post-BPR: A Leaner, Faster, Change-Oriented Workplace

While BreakPoint BPR emphasizes business processes, the changes it creates change the face—and the pace—of the entire operation. Every enterprise develops its own unique post-BPR environment, but a pattern of paradigm shifts—radical changes in the way work gets done—are characteristic. Key changes include new ways of working with customers and suppliers, new ways of using information systems, and newly empowered workers.

Strategic Alliances with Customers and Suppliers

BPR strategies often go beyond the process to involve those at either end of that process: the customer and the suppli-er. The BPR premise that customers and suppliers are part of the cross-functional core business process is more than rhetoric. The perspective has led to rethinking where processes should begin and where they should end.

For example, the Fibers Division of Allied-Signal Corpora-tion discovered that custom-making specific fiber products for key customers, such as carpet manufacturers, could increase their potential for sales. But closer cooperation and coordina-tion between Allied Fibers and the customers would be essen-tial.

To take advantage of the opportunity, a BPR team redesigned key processes around these products, and the customers gave Allied Fibers preferred supplier status. The new alliance reduced cycle time and costs for the carpet manufacturers, while producing more, and more regular, business for Allied Fibers. The extended fiber-to-carpet process also got a new, more seamless look, replacing the discrete series of interactions the old approach involved. At Allied Fibers, the cycle time was reduced from 16 weeks to two, thus allowing for premium pricing at the point of sale—a major breakthrough in the new alliance.

The same logic can hold on the other side of the equation. Medrad, a fast-growing, $60 million medical imaging company, developed a strategic alliance with one of its preferred shippers as part of a process redesign of its customer order process. Previously, Medrad had used a variety of carriers for shipping its disposable product line. Preparing orders for shipping caused major delays, and they had no ability to meet customer demands for "rush" shipments.

Under a new partnership arrangement, the shipper now carries most Medrad disposable product shipments. The shipper supplied the computer hardware and software both partners use to schedule and track shipments. Close communication and common information via computer allows a smoother, streamlined order-to-ship process for both partners. The results? On-time delivery improved for Medrad from 86 percent to 100 percent in the first six months. Order processing costs were cut in half, and customer complaints went from 150 to 0 per month.

Sometimes strategic alliances cause the customer or the supplier to take on part of the other company's role. Owens-Corning Fiberglass, for example, decided to perform some tasks itself that were traditionally the carrier's responsibility. The company now positions the trailers the carrier delivers to the manufacturing plant and loads them itself according to job site destination. Completing this part of the job not only saves money, it also gives Owens-Corning Fiberglass more control in

FIGURE 3-1

BREAKPOINT BPR CHANGES
MORE THAN PROCESSES

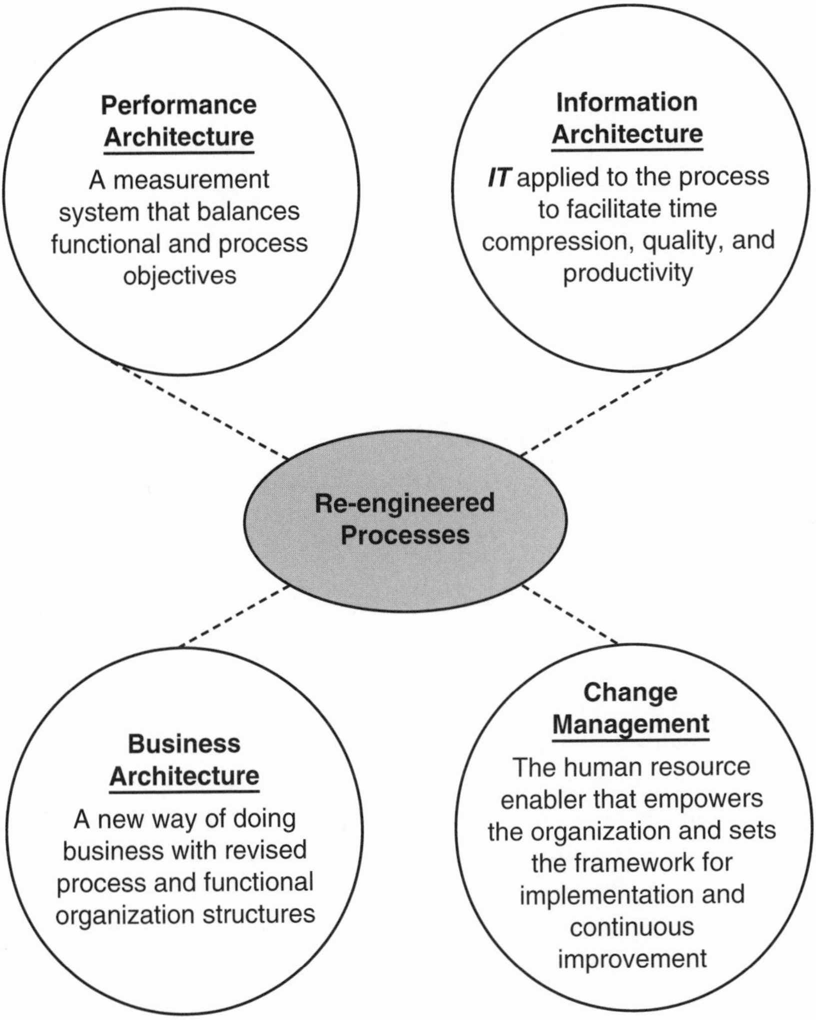

Performance Architecture

A measurement system that balances functional and process objectives

Information Architecture

IT applied to the process to facilitate time compression, quality, and productivity

Re-engineered Processes

Business Architecture

A new way of doing business with revised process and functional organization structures

Change Management

The human resource enabler that empowers the organization and sets the framework for implementation and continuous improvement providing dependable job site deliveries to its customers.

Banks have used the opposite approach: getting customers to do some jobs that used to require bank employees. Thanks to the clever use of technology, customers can now withdraw, deposit, and transfer funds themselves, cutting down on staffing needs and making the customer an integral part of the cash-to-cash process.

Outsourcing is another approach that looks beyond internal capabilities to get the job done. Some companies have found that contracting out functions traditionally performed in-house can both save money and make a process more efficient. Bankers Trust, for example, has outsourced almost every function not central to its core business, including employee orientation. A southern bank saved $25 million in technology costs by contracting for the services.

Using Information Systems To Support New Ways of Working

While automation itself is not necessarily part of the picture in a post-BPR environment, information technology (IT) often enables completely new ways of doing the job. For example, the Frito-Lay Company, like many other businesses with field staff, has given its route salespeople easy-to-use laptop computers. They use the portable machines to input customer orders directly, which allows orders to be filled correctly with fewer processing steps.

It can do more than enable process redesign; sometimes it's the essential factor in completely transforming a process. The experience of Walgreen Drug illustrates the role information technology can have in business process redesign. Strategic analysis had suggested to Walgreen executives that inventory management could be a new profit driver. To exploit this advantage, they developed a real-time inventory control system, the means of capturing and automating prescription management, and an infrastructure to link these together. By integrating these previously separate operational capabilities, they gave customers a service that created a market: the ability to fill and refill prescriptions from any Walgreen store. This convenience translated to customer loyalty, repeat sales, and increased revenues.

John Moore, writing in *Systems and Network Integration,* describes several types of technologies that can help companies change the way they do business. Client/server technology, for example, allows companies to make data available organization-wide. Companies can decentralize or get closer to the customer and still have access to the information they need to make decisions. Document management and imaging products also let companies change the job, not just automate it.

"This situation is markedly different from the 1970's mini-computer revolution that let companies simply automate existing departments," Moore writes. "Today technology can spark a corporate makeover."

Empowering the Worker

Quite often, workers in a post-BPR environment have more responsible roles in redesigned processes. This change is in line with modern management thinking about the benefits of employee participation, and often it may be necessary for effective process operations.

For example, individuals may be given more authority, as in a case reported by the Conference Board. A high-tech manu-facturer empowered its field sales representatives to make quotations and process orders and its warehouse personnel to approve and process credit memos. Previously, getting managerial sign-offs was a standard part of these jobs. Now, information systems provide the facts, policies, or models employees need to make these decisions.

Changing from traditional management to a team approach is another way of empowering employees after BPR. Organizing around outcomes, not tasks; matching authority and responsibility; and pushing accountability downwards are hall-marks of this approach.

At General Foods, after the redesign of the product development process, cross-functional teams led key tasks. The team approach reduced time-to-market by as much as 50 per-cent. A components manufacturing division of Kodak found that empowering workers and using teams has enabled one shift to do what used to require three. In a financial services compa-ny, self-managed teams now perform each step in "their" trans-action and are held accountable for completing all such transactions within a specified geographic area. In its first year, reported the *McKinsey Quarterly,* work volume at the financial services company increased by 17 percent and staffing levels declined by 13 percent.

As these examples of change suggest, the post-BPR com-pany is often a smaller company with fewer people, fewer facil-ities, less floor space and inventory, fewer management layers, and fewer managers. Organizational learning—especially learn-ing how to do things differently—becomes a significant corpo-rate value. The post-BPR organization has learned how to change concurrently in all the business disciplines, and respond-ing flexibly to change has become a way of life.

Summary

- Both the way work is done and the work environment change radically after BPR, which means establishing new strategic alliances with customers and suppliers and involving them in new roles and responsibilities.

- New information technology is not a necessary part of BPR, but it can be an important enabler of new work models. The best use of this technology is in creating a transformation to new, different, and effective process operations, not in automating existing ones.

- The workplace after BPR is a leaner, more focused,

more challenging environment that is readier to compete in a changing market. Fewer employees may be involved in specific processes, and they are empowered to contribute more—often as members of a cross-functional team.

SECTION 2

Making BPR Work: Essential Factors for Success

BPR affects every aspect of an organization. To succeed, a BPR project must address the context within which process change occurs: an organization's culture and expectations; the framework of the BPR project itself; and the forces that drive, shape, and support new directions.

This section discusses five key factors that receive as much attention in Coopers & Lybrand's BreakPoint BPR as business processes themselves:

◆

Assessing customers, competitors, and capabilities

◆

Getting the right people involved in BPR

◆

Using information technology in the right way

◆

Managing organizational change

◆

Following through with continuous improvement

These issues are a high priority because how a company handles them can make or break its BPR effort.

51

CHAPTER 4

ASSESSING CUSTOMERS, COMPETITORS, AND CAPABILITIES

CHAPTER HIGHLIGHTS

◆

How PHH FleetAmerica used strategic assessment
to define its competitive breakpoint.

◆

Strategic assessment for BreakPoint BPR
includes four analyses:

1. Needs of customers and shareholders.

2. Competitor strengths and weaknesses,
and overall market conditions.

3. Capabilities of the company to make dramatic changes.

4. Economic implications of strategic alternatives.

PHH FleetAmerica: Answering Aggressive Competition with Client-Driven Change

A few years ago, corporate giant General Electric (GE) acquired four vehicle fleet management companies, creating formidable competition for PHH FleetAmerica, a $2 billion unit of PHH Corporation. GE's reputation for aggressiveness and innovation (plus deep pockets) meant industry leader PHH FleetAmerica had to develop some breakthroughs fast—or face a dismal future.

Fleet management includes a variety of services: setting policy for automobile and truck use; acquiring and delivering vehicles; vehicle maintenance; managing related funds, tax and title concerns; information management; and even paying traffic tickets. "An organization starts out with a basic choice about these activities: do them in-house, or contract them out to a firm like ours," says Jim Prebil, PHH FleetAmerica's senior vice president for strategic resources. "So we have to show clients that we can provide better service, value, and cost savings than they would gain from the in-house alternative."

What is the bedrock of this type of business? Without hesitation, Prebil answers, "Understanding and responding to clients' ever-changing needs. To be a leader in this industry, everyone in your company has to be extremely customer-focused. That's PHH FleetAmerica's foundation, and when the challenge came from GE, we drew on the strength of that legacy." PHH FleetAmerica's response to the challenge began with extensive research, including:

- Conducting an in-depth survey of all major fleet management services clients—PHH's own and those served by competitors. As part of the research, clients ranked PHH and other providers on 89 different attributes of fleet management.

- Convening client focus groups to probe for unmet service needs and "wish lists."

- Developing a model, based on detailed client-value criteria, to help pinpoint service lapses and opportunities. The model also allowed PHH to analyze the impact of proposed changes before making final decisions.

This provided valuable information about PHH's performance in the eyes of clients, and also revealed competitors' strengths and weaknesses. PHH added to this strategic assessment by benchmarking its approaches to doing business against those of other best-in-class companies.

Based on this research, PHH is using BPR in redesigning its core business processes—the operations that mean the most to clients. For example, PHH is re-engineering its vendor selection and vehicle ordering process to give clients access to the best possible network of auto sales and service dealers, gasoline service stations, and repair shops. The breakthrough: this valued-added dealer network will help PHH continue to offer lower-cost services than competitors, and enhance quality control in a very visible aspect of fleet vehicle management.

But what is and is not visible depends on customer perceptions. Prebil recalls, "One of our discoveries was that clients were dissatisfied with the fleet vehicle management industry's low-tech, fragmented approach to basic services. For example, we thought of ordering and billing as operations that were 'invisible' to clients, but these processes turned out to matter a great deal to their perception of value received. We realized that radical changes here would improve customer perceptions of PHH services and create a substantial competitive advantage."

In its old billing model, PHH assembled the dozens and even hundreds of invoices the company received from its dealer network and internal operations, and sent clients hard copies of them along with a bill. PHH's redesign of the process is a new, high-tech billing procedure that fully integrates ordering, vehi-

55

cle maintenance, and accounts receivable. The breakthrough: a client can receive a single bill that includes a listing and reconciliation of all related services.

"We chose BPR as the route to making these types of breakthroughs because PHH cannot afford a more gradual approach at this time," says Prebil. "GE has already completed a process improvement approach designed to give them a substantial competitive edge by introducing new technologies. But it took them years and millions of dollars in incremental investments. With a redesign effort that is faster, more comprehensive, and more flexible than GE's, we have the opportunity to leapfrog ahead of them."

BreakPoint BPR:
Starting from Strategy, not Scratch

PHH is an example of a company that is conducting BPR at its most dynamic, breakpoint level. The company conducted the kinds of strategic assessment activities that showed them where they stood in relation to their competitors and their market. Because the goal of BreakPoint BPR is gaining a competitive edge, the ability to make this type of comparison is fundamental to success. Strategic assessment for BPR looks at operations, technical, and environmental conditions to plan change. Core business process analysis then links the activities of an operation to its strategic objectives.

Instead of relying solely on traditional structural methods of competitive positioning, such as market segmentation or product positioning, strategic assessment for BreakPoint BPR revisits customer and shareholder expectations, market dynamics, the role of information, and the business's core capabilities. All of these factors must be fully understood to identify a breakpoint advantage. To obtain this information, BreakPoint BPR projects focus on four types of analyses:

    1. A comprehensive understanding of the needs and preferences of customers and shareholders.

2. A thorough environmental and competitor analysis.

3. An objective analysis of the resources and capabilities of the organization.

4. Quantitative information that allows modeling of the economic implications of strategic alternatives.

1. Finding Out What Customers Really Want

BreakPoint BPR involves an intense focus on customers. Market research, through surveys, focus groups, or customer advisory panels like PHH uses, provides an external vision of quality and value. As noted in Chapter 2, this information is critical to giving BPR projects the capability to produce the right kinds of dramatic change.

"BPR projects can and often do proceed without taking this step," says Coopers & Lybrand's Grady Means. "But when a project overlooks this aspect of strategic assessment, it lacks necessary information for identifying competitive advantage." A company can use BPR to achieve considerable cost reduction or cycle time improvement without this information. But it may still fail to improve its competitive position if the changes mean nothing to customers.

Not just any customer will do for this type of assessment. Most organizations base their research on the broad, undifferentiated mass of their customers. For example, according to *Fortune* magazine, when Hewlett Packard developed the first hand-held calculator for engineers and scientists, the company's customer research said there was no market for it: the slide rule worked fine. Often, it's better to focus on your "barometric" customers—those who are on the leading edge, with the vision to respond to innovation and anticipate change. When you look for breakthroughs, their opinions are most important.

PHH FleetAmerica uses pilot projects so that clients react to the real, not the abstract. Says Prebil, "You often need to show clients a new idea, not just tell them about it. That's why some of our innovation development includes a pilot test to see how clients respond. For example, we are pilot testing innovations such as on-board data transfer, door-to-door delivery of vehicles to help clients avoid loss of productivity, and vehicle maintenance in customer parking lots. Once customers see a new concept at work, they are better able to suggest modifications and enhancements that increase the value of the idea."

2. Understanding the Competition and the Marketplace

"You can't boost your competitive position without understanding the external environment in which you operate," says Grady Means. "Information about customers and shareholders is critical, but it is only half of the equation. The other half is solid data about your competition, market conditions, and exemplary industry practices."

While significant process improvements can result from focusing only on internal conditions, you can't catch or overtake your competitors unless you know where they are in the race. Detailed knowledge of their strengths and weaknesses can help you identify where your company's competitive edge may lie. To complete the picture, you also need to understand the dynamics of your overall market, another critical consideration in finding a breakpoint advantage.

Looking at the Market

When a looming glut in the market for the basic stock form of polyvinyl chloride (PVC) threatened to cut prices by 50 percent, for example, the Geon Vinyl Division of BF Goodrich knew it was time for a change. They made a strategic decision to get out of the unprofitable basic stock PVC business and become a custom maker of specialty plastic compounds. "The opportunities were greater there," Bruce Gordon, the company's BPR coordinator, told *Information Week*. "Other aspects of the competitive environment also made this line of business appealing. Some of our larger competitors aren't in this market, the profit margins are larger, and it is less vulnerable to economic downturns."

This strategic vision and information about their market prompted a comprehensive BPR effort. It also helped identify the kinds of changes that would make Geon Vinyl a strong competitor.

"To beat the competition in the specialty plastics arena, we had to have 100 percent on-time delivery," Gordon notes. "We have come close to reaching that goal by redesigning our order, production and distribution processes. Before, we made a product and stored it in our warehouses until customers ordered it. Now, we make it as soon as customers place their order, and deliver it to them immediately. This allows more accurate scheduling, and it also gives us a cost advantage by reducing inventory."

Companies get information on the competition and the market in several ways. Like PHH, they survey their competitors' customers to get their perspective on strengths and weaknesses. Trade associations, survey research firms, Chambers of Commerce, and advisory panels can also provide information. Also, astute organizations use their sales force to gather intelligence on what competitors are marketing to customers. Often, this is a company's "first-alert" to rival products and securities. The first key to this practice is to listen to what the sales force reports (too often, they are ignored). The second is to reward this sleuthing to reinforce the value of it.

Benchmarking

Benchmarking is another essential tool for strategically driven BPR. In her book, *Benchmarking,* Coopers & Lybrand managing associate Kathleen Leibfried defines benchmarking as the art of looking at "existing processes or activities and then identify[ing] an external point or reference or standard by which that activity can be measured or judged." The book also features this definition by David Kearns, former CEO of Xerox: "The continuous process of measuring product, services, and practices against the toughest competitors, or those companies recognized as industry leaders."

Benchmarking may involve comparisons at three levels: internally, comparing performance of similar units or divisions; within an industry; or with the "best-in-class" performance of a function from any industry. Such comparison is essential to a company's strategic vision, and it is also useful in setting priorities for redesign. Knowing how competitors and best-in-class performers have designed their processes can help in visualizing "what if" breakthrough scenarios.

For example, Exxon Chemical, a multi-billion dollar division of Exxon Corporation, used benchmarking in its radical redesign of the information services (IS) development and support processes. They looked at both of their competitors and international companies in other industries for whom IS competency is or can become a competitive edge. Ultimately, they reorganized the IS processes, moving away from their predominantly centralized structure to the decentralized model used by companies with profiles similar to Exxon. They applied the experience others had in using technological innovations to set their own priorities for system changes, and they developed ideas for maximizing the strategic use of data already in service. Without this external view, their understanding of what was possible and what was essential would have been superficial at best.

3. An Objective Appraisal of Capabilities

As the example in Chapter 1 discussed, knowledge of their external environment helped the Bendix Automotive Systems Group of Allied-Signal identify a major competitive opportunity in the anti-lock brakes market. But a critical question remained to be answered: Did the company have the capability to get the brake systems to market within the required time frame?

While it is important not to limit creative vision in Break-Point BPR, a redesign goal must also be reality-based. Yes, BPR can change old processes, introduce new technologies, and make the most of core competencies. But do critical barriers exist within your overall operations, supplier network, or culture that will hold you back?

Business performance appraisal can help companies objectively assess their capacity for change and how far improvement strategies should reach. During BreakPoint BPR project planning, the company will determine which of the following aspects of business performance appraisal need to be done, who will conduct the reviews, and the level of detail required.

- **Financial review.** Analysis of financial and management accounts to identify and explain significant trends and implications and to define an operational base case.

- **Operational review.** Assessment and explanation of the operational efficiency and effectiveness of the company's functions. While this review should cover all functions, sometimes it is focused on functions that quick mapping (see Chapter 9) or strategic assessment have proven to offer the best opportunities.

- **Information management review.** Assessment of the current and future role of information services and the extent to which it can provide support to core business processes.

- **Key performance indicators.** Investigation of the quality and coverage of management information flows within the organization. In particular, performance indicators are used in monitoring core processes and organizational behavior.

- **Cultural assessment.** This is a review of the aspects

of an organization's culture—its values, norms, and beliefs—that will help promote, and perhaps resist, the major changes brought about by BPR. We discuss this type of assessment at length in Chapter 7.

These appraisals document and explain the company's overall financial, operational, and cultural performance, both good and bad. They ensure that nothing of importance to the redesign process is overlooked, and it produces information that helps focus the redesign appropriately, such as:

- A list of short-term opportunities for improving business performance. By identifying sources of immediate financial savings, BPR effort can help "pay for itself."

- A statement of the company's current financial position (i.e., profit and loss account, balance sheets, and cash-flow statements).

- A list of processes that are "broken" in financial terms (produced in conjunction with the quick map) and a translation of financial performance measures into process performance measures. While BPR takes a cross-functional view of processes, the more traditional review conducted here may reveal exceptional strengths and weaknesses in individual functions that can have important implications for BPR. For example, high staff turnover in the sales function may well be associated with high levels of rework in the order fulfillment process, suggesting a redesign that improves both.

- A list of infrastructure constraints on radical change (a new factory or warehouse that would be politically hard to close or an expensive new information system the company expects the BPR effort to use, rather than replace).

- A list of gaps in management information, including situations in which existing information and performance measures drive behavior toward functional optimization at the expense of cross-functional process performance.

- An indication of how employees and managers will respond to major changes, and what must be done to align the organization's culture with the principles and values required in radically different working environments.

4. Analyzing the Economic Impact of Change

When PHH FleetAmerica developed potential innovations for one of its core business processes, a key task was projecting the costs and benefits of making changes. One idea considered was using autonomous teams of workers, instead of continuing the practice of direct supervision by managers.

"Was it financially viable to use work teams to conduct part of this process? We needed good cost data to be sure," recalls Prebil. "On the cost side, we identified $200,000. On the benefit side, we projected $2.6 million in direct benefits and $500,000 in indirect benefits. This translated into a net present value of $1.5 million. These figures gave us more confidence in moving ahead with work teams. By conducting this kind of financial analysis for all proposed changes to a core business process, we are able to forecast the total costs and benefits of redesigning it."

BreakPoint BPR: Beyond Process Improvement

Strategic-level activities such as these separate BreakPoint BPR from traditional process improvement. They are a critical foundation for the breakthrough-level changes described in Chapters 1–3.

BPR efforts that revamp a large, transfunctional process, or redesign a process to maximize use of a new technology can produce valuable benefits—and may be all you need. But if your goal is closing or creating a competitive gap, strategic activities are essential. While no set formula exists for creating a breakthrough, a strategic perspective and the supports discussed in Chapters 5–8 make BreakPoint BPR more than process improvement or re-engineering. For many companies, it can be a competitive advantage now as well as in the future.

Summary

- BreakPoint BPR can take companies beyond process improvement. It operates at a strategic level, and competitive advantage is its goal.

- Some BPR projects are large-scale, cross-functional process improvement programs. While they can be beneficial, strategic-level BreakPoint BPR has the greatest potential to close competitive gaps and create market leaders.

- To understand customer needs, it's important to ask customers what they want. They may need your help to envision innovations that would delight them.

- Solid data about your competition, market conditions, and best-in-class industry practices is critical to finding your breakpoint advantage.

- Business performance appraisal helps companies assess their capacity for dramatic change.

- Economic impact analyses show whether business process changes will actually improve the company's competitive position. Potential financial impact is a key consideration in deciding what to change.

CHAPTER 5

GETTING THE RIGHT PEOPLE INVOLVED

CHAPTER HIGHLIGHTS

◆

How one company staffed and organized
a global breakthrough project.

◆

Choosing the right staff for BPR:
getting the right mix of personal qualities and specialized skills.

◆

The roles chairmen, board members, senior managers,
middle managers, and employees play in BPR.

◆

How BPR is organized and managed as a project.

◆

The roles consultants can play—and what to look for
in selecting one.

BPR: Whom Do Companies Involve?

This story is told of Werner von Braun, a pioneer of America's space program. Someone once found him lying on the beach at Cape Canaveral, staring out at the waves. "What are you thinking about, Dr. von Braun? Are you dreaming about an innovation in space flight, or how to solve some problem?"

"No," he replied. "I am thinking about something much more important: my team."

Just so, one of the most important decisions you will make in a BPR project is how to staff and support the teams that will run it. One challenge: capture the right skills and personal characteristics needed for the project. Another: choose people who will help win support for the new way of working.

One international company with whom Coopers & Lybrand works took a multi-level, cross-functional team approach to meet these twin challenges. At the start, the company formed an executive steering committee to provide strategic guidance and to coordinate BPR projects. This group included top managers from the key departments involved in the processes to be redesigned, and functions such as finance, legal, sales, and information systems. Senior management participation at this stage sent a clear message that executives took redesign seriously.

Next, the company formed design teams to focus on specific business processes. A design team always included staff who worked in the process undergoing redesign, who brought aboard an intimate knowledge of operations. Also, their participation helped win support from their colleagues in the process. In-house information technology specialists chosen for their creativity and understanding of corporate processes rounded out the team. BPR consultants from Coopers & Lybrand supported and trained the design teams in process mapping, computer simulation of redesign options, and facilitated the creative side of a project. Such teams became the workhorses of BPR, mapping and modeling the existing process and developing recommendations for new ones.

"This team structure is what makes BPR projects successful," says Helen Ojha, a Coopers & Lybrand partner specializing in information technology. "Executives set policy and direction, and staff provide specialized knowledge about a process, your business, customers, and information technology. From the top of an organization on down, you involve people in making changes that they otherwise might resist. And when you need them, you use consultants with expertise and training in BPR tools and techniques and other areas that are new to an organization."

Just like von Braun, the higher up you are on the organizational chart, the more time you must spend on guiding the team aspects of BPR. Having the 'right' people do a redesign is more important than having any single 'right' solution.

The Breakthrough Team: Who Are the Right People?

Who in the company should be involved in BPR?

What kind of staff commitment does it take?

Questions like these are of major interest to companies considering BPR; the just-mentioned example shows how one company answered them. As in any important business project, paying close attention to staffing issues is essential. Involving the right people, at the right times, and in the most effective ways can make the difference between success and failure of BPR efforts.

Staffing

"A company usually envisions three choices in staffing a redesign process," notes Helen Ojha. "First, they could have a 'Superman' fly in from outside and do the redesign for them. When he flies back to the North Pole, however, they could be left with a plan that doesn't fit their company and that no one has a stake in carrying out.

"Second, they might develop an internal staff team to conduct BPR. The plan they produced would fit the company but it might be impossible to find the in-house BPR expertise to carry it out.

"Third, they could have internal people work with BPR experts to develop an overall plan, and charge the people currently responsible for specific functions with redesigning those functions. This approach can work, but only if people work together in cross-functional teams and focus on improving a total business process. Our international client successfully used this model."

While each BPR project needs a tailored staffing plan, the organizational elements in Figure 5-1 are common to most efforts. Each company will place managers with different titles in each circle shown in the figure, depending on the focus of the project and on which managers are their strongest leaders, regardless of specialty. The size of teams will also vary depending on the scope of the redesign. However, staffing plans for successful projects have three characteristics in common:

The highest executive has a leadership role, and senior managers play prominent parts. In most successful efforts, the CEO, the president, or the chief financial officer (CFO) champions BPR throughout the organization. The importance of top executive support was underlined in a recent Conference Board survey. Respondents ranked "obtaining executive involvement/support" as by far the most important factor in instituting BPR.

The priority management support received in the survey is understandable because only the highest levels of management can make the wide-ranging decisions that BPR requires. Their involvement also sends signals to middle managers and employees that the company is serious about dramatic change.

This support can take many forms. In the Bank of Boston example in Chapter 1, the CFO created a new management team to spearhead change and innovation. At the major insurance company discussed in Chapter 3, the CEO took organizational steps to ensure the priority of BPR. For example, when one of the senior executives first suggested that a "case manager" could handle all the tasks in a complex insurance process, the CEO "not only supported the idea, he wanted to use it on the company's most important process, underwriting and issue," a former executive recalls. "Because of his support, some of our other managers started to get excited about the possibilities. When the human resources group threw up barriers because the case manager concept was completely alien to their job categories and career paths, the CEO gave them an immediate reason to get on board. He put human resources under me."

The company's "best and brightest" people must participate in BPR. Dramatic change requires people with creativity, vision, and openness to innovation. Often, they will already be some of the busiest people in a company because everyone recognizes and respects their talents. Yet they are made available to BPR because top management gives this assignment a high priority.

For example, Bill Adler, president of PHH FleetAmerica, wanted Jim Prebil to head the company's BPR effort. At the time, Prebil was very involved in his own job as vice president for human resources for all of PHH Corporation. Adler had to make a strong case to PHH board of directors chairman Bob Kunisch that Prebil's participation was critical to the company's strategic BPR initiatives. Says Adler, "When the chairman said

FIGURE 5-1

BPR: WHO'S INVOLVED?

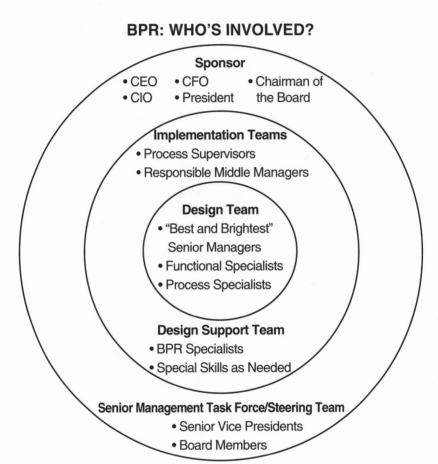

Sponsor
- CEO
- CIO
- CFO
- President
- Chairman of the Board

Implementation Teams
- Process Supervisors
- Responsible Middle Managers

Design Team
- "Best and Brightest" Senior Managers
- Functional Specialists
- Process Specialists

Design Support Team
- BPR Specialists
- Special Skills as Needed

Senior Management Task Force/Steering Team
- Senior Vice Presidents
- Board Members

FIGURE 5-1 (Continued)

Design Team:
Maps the "as-is" process
Creates the redesign
Plans for implementation
Owns the redesign process and outcomes
Advocates breakpoint changes
Oversees and coordinates the design process

Design Support Group:
Works with design team to help manage the effort
Provides relevant experience in BPR methodologies and technical issues
Helps facilitate breakthrough thinking leading to radical redesign
Forms focused networks of special interests, experience, or skills as
    needed in analysis and design

Implementation:
Carry out implementation plans
Set new performance indicators

Sponsor:
Sets overall direction/vision
Allocates resources
Resolves policy issues
Approves plans
Champions change
Assures team training/skills

Senior Management Task Force:
Defines scope of redesign
Aligns BPR with strategic goals/objectives
Defines breakpoint
Defines BPR goals/objectives
Provides resources
Tracks performance
Approves plans
Champions changes

'Yes,' he was doing more than giving us Jim's time. He was demonstrating commitment from the top, and that has cascaded down through every level of our organization."

This commitment enabled Prebil to assemble the best possible BPR team: "I recruited the people that managers were *least* willing to lose," recalls Prebil, "which made an enormous difference. The high caliber of our BPR team allowed us to accomplish in months what could have taken years."

The project teams include a cross-functional mix of the practical and technical perspectives required for change. Important elements usually include operations, finance, information services, corporate strategy, human resources, and knowledge and experience with BPR tools and techniques.

Other important contributors. Ideally, an organization should have a bias toward maximizing participation of all those who will be affected by a major change. Getting company-wide input from senior and middle managers and other employees who are not on top-level BPR teams is particularly important in shaping project plans. Ways to get this input include personal interviews, interactive workshops, and focus group interviews, which can help in:

- Describing an as-is process
- Assessing/defining corporate strategy
- Appraising current performance and organizational fitness
- Describing the corporate culture and identifying key change management issues
- Validating/reality-checking a BPR vision

Remember that if you ask for ideas, you should respond to

suggestions you receive. This means sharing the final plan with all contributors and explaining why you rejected some of their suggestions.

Time

How much time does it take to make a BPR breakthrough? For simple business processes confined to a few functions, it can be as short as two or three months—provided the people in the process are ready and able to change (see Chapter 7 for more on this readiness). For a major change involving many functions and perhaps the whole organization, the implementation may take a couple of years (however, the initial planning period is much shorter).

Simple or complex, a breakthrough is a major change initiative that requires focused attention:

- Members of the initial design team should count on a full-time commitment during the process-mapping and creative planning phases, which usually take no more than three to four months.

- The sponsor/senior management steering team will have a heavy involvement initially in planning the BPR project, but will have less intensive review and decision-making responsibilities thereafter.

- Smaller teams responsible for sub-processes may be active for 6 months or more, particularly if the redesign is phased in function-by-function or department-by-department.

BreakPoint BPR is a full-time commitment for Coopers & Lybrand personnel who staff design support teams and assist with project management. However, our functional/technical specialists, like their client counterparts, participate on an as-needed basis. Usually, our work is done after a few months,

Helping BPR Teams Succeed:
Practical Pointers

- For continuity, create core teams that will participate throughout the BPR process. You can get special skills you need on a short-term basis by forming *ad hoc* project teams to complete discrete tasks. And while the core of participants should remain the same, the project structure can change as needed.

- Choose team members with experience in strategic visioning, change management, and team improvement initiatives. People with varied backgrounds, even those without direct experience in the core process to be changed, are important because they can generate new insights and challenge the status quo more rigorously.

- Balance creative and change management skills on a team.

- Make sure that internal or external BPR support team staff think through "blue sky" ideas in advance of creative sessions. This will "seed" brainstorming for even more creative solutions.

- Give your teams the power to change anything as they develop objectives and designs.

- Give your teams the training they need to conduct BPR activities effectively. Examples include training in how to use simulation tools, process-mapping, and group decision techniques.

- Build commitment to the redesign by involving people with credibility and influence in your company—at all levels of authority and across all units.

- Tap in-house expertise, such as that in the training and human resources departments. Training and personnel issues will arise in each phase of BPR, and involving the company experts can facilitate your process.

- Conduct team-building workshops/events if needed to bring teammembers together and overcome barriers to cooperation.

- Be prepared to add outside suppliers and even customers to teams when their input adds value to the BPR project.

although some clients ask us to stay on throughout the implementation phase.

Managing the BPR Project

BPR is a temporary job, which means it can have an *ad hoc* management structure. Exactly which structure you choose should depend on the nature of the change you plan. However, your goal is to create a management plan that will get the job done; personal or political considerations should not dictate your choices.

Who Leads the Effort?

One of the key personnel decisions in a BPR project is who should manage and coordinate the effort within the company. While it is important that the BPR project manager be a senior manager with the authority to get things done, his/her corporate title will vary in every company. In the international trading project discussed above, the project manager was a managing director from one of the operational units involved. At the Xerox Corporation, the director of business process integration heads a 14-person Business Process Board that coordinates projects. At PHH FleetAmerica, the job went to the senior vice president for human resources.

While information services executives participate in BPR, a recent *Information Week* issue on the subject made a strong case against their leading or managing the effort. The principal reason: they don't have a broad enough constituency to influence change. *Information Week*'s leading candidate is the head of the business group that owns the process to be redesigned, such as the vice president of operations or a business unit vice president.

Qualities to look for in a BPR project director. In Coopers & Lybrand's experience, BPR efforts need a "champion," someone with superior leadership and management skills who has, through position and track record, strong organizational credibility. As a leader, the project director will need to help create and communicate a vision of what the company redesign can achieve through BPR. He or she also needs the ability to choose the right people for teams and motivate them to take the right actions. Finally, the job requires enthusiasm for the cause of major improvement, and a tremendous amount of hard work.

As a manager, the project director's challenge will be to monitor and coordinate complex tasks, but with a flexible attitude and the capability to respond to the needs of the day. In managing a BPR project, flexibility is a more important quality than being a stick-to-schedule taskmaster. As discussed in Chapter 9, the original plan will—and should—be changed over the course of the project. The project director and the management system must adjust quickly.

Planners Are More Important Than the Plan

The first task in project management is developing a comprehensive project plan that defines the work to be done and ensures sufficient resources. In an effective project, the plan does not gather dust on a shelf; it is the baseline for managing activities and measuring progress. It must also be a living document that changes over time to reflect the current situation.

At first, top-level team managers will create a high level plan that covers the complete BPR process. Keeping the plan at a high level initially is important because the BPR process demands the flexibility to set direction on the basis of analyses completed at various steps. Along the way, you may also encounter major problems or discover new opportunities that change your task or your timeline. Thus, our experience suggests that phase-by-phase details should not be developed until several months in advance of taking action.

As General Dwight D. Eisenhower said when he commanded the Allied Forces in World War II: "Plans are nothing. Planning is everything." He would have made a great BPR pro-

---

Keys to BPR Management

- Choose your most effective managers who know how to lead people and coordinate large-scale, cross-functional efforts.

- Maintain a focus on business objectives when day-to-day snarls or setbacks occur. In any major change, things get worse before they get better.

- Make proactive decisions. Effective BPR cannot happen by accident.

- Oversee all activities without getting bogged down in administrative detail or the micromanagement of individual projects.

- Communicate regularly and effectively with managers and employees working on the project and throughout the organization.

---

ject manager. He knew that regularly bringing together key people to create and update plans was more important than having a static document called "the plan." It is the interaction of these people—their discussions and consensus building—that creates a dynamic plan everyone can support.

Implementation

One of the biggest management challenges occurs in the implementation phase of the BPR project, which involves coordinating a number of simultaneous, but very different, changes to:

- Processes
- Information systems
- Organizational structures
- Performance measures
- Behavior and values

Internal or external consultant support is usually required to apply the variety of disciplines needed to plan and oversee this wide-ranging group of tasks.

Involving Consultants Effectively

Should your BPR effort use outside consultants or rely completely on internal staffing? The answer to this question depends on how you prefer to get the resources and expertise you will need to conduct redesign, including:

- Knowledge of the methodologies, tools, and techniques used in BPR

- Experience with other BPR efforts in your industry

- Time to devote to the tasks

Some companies may have these resources in-house or choose to develop them. Others prefer to supplement internal resources by involving consultants. A 1992 report that Coopers & Lybrand commissioned from G2 Research, Inc., gives some insight into current and future industry practices. The study included interviews with 30 Fortune 1000 CEOs and 100 chief information officers (CIOs) or heads of management information system departments.

- About two-thirds of Fortune 1000 companies that engage in BPR do so without outside assistance. However, most of these companies do not conduct market research or collect any other external data before starting their redesigns. According to G2: "The result is that they reinforce their own opinions, create paper plans that are never implemented, and often generate internal friction and resentment in the process."

- Of the one-third of the corporations that did use consultants, in 1992 about 68 percent of BPR costs were esti-

78

mated to be internal to the companies, while 32 percent paid for external expertise and support services. The report projects that by 1997, 58 percent of costs will be internal, and 42 percent external. One reason for the projected increase in use of external resources, says G2, is that, while top-notch consultants cost more than internal staff, "they bring a knowledge of the market environment, the competition, and the most recent information technologies to the table, without internal bias or politics." Another reason may be that corporate downsizing and the practice of outsourcing means that companies have fewer people to spare for the temporary task of business process redesign.

If you decide to invest in outside consultants, it is critical that you select and use them the right way. Here are some guidelines, based on our experience and on the special requirements of BPR projects.

The Role of the Consultant

If your company decides to work with outside consultants, what roles should they play? Many companies have found that it is effective to use consultants as:

- **Coaches,** who can offer leadership, encouragement, and an experience-based assessment of what it will take to "win" with BPR.

- **Facilitators,** who use proven tools and techniques to keep the change process running smoothly.

- **Visionaries,** who can focus more freely on the future because they are experienced innovators—and because they have no stake in the past.

- **Experts,** who have the knowledge and skills to conduct BPR.

- **Project management assistants,** who have the time, the tools, and the experience to coordinate diverse, broad sets of corporate-wide activities.

- **Trainers,** who can quickly instruct client staff in the day-to-day BPR skills they need, such as process-mapping and simulation, using statistical improvement tools in process design and measurement, and visioning.

Finally, effective consultants will not "do" BPR to your organization, nor should you want them to. Instead, they will work in partnership with you and your people to maximize breakthrough results.

Choosing a Consultant

The checklist in the box suggests some important factors to keep in mind when choosing a consultant. By the end of 1991, almost 80 consulting firms offered some kind of BPR services, which probably vary greatly in quality and capability. Remember, as a distinct methodology, BPR is only a few years old and is still developing. Make sure companies can back up their claims to expertise with the appropriate experience and credentials.

BPR and Systems Re-engineering

Systems re-engineering covers a wide variety of areas, from basic systems planning to converting existing software code from old programming languages to new ones. Smart organizations understand that BPR and systems re-engineering often go hand-in-hand. The next chapter discusses this interrelatedness at length, and Figure 5-2 illustrates it. Unfortunately, very few consulting firms and systems companies are experienced in both areas. According to G2: "For the growing body of users who want end-to-end service, this narrows the competitive choice considerably."

You can use two consulting firms for the same job, one an

Choosing a Consultant: A Checklist

To be sure you are getting a
well-qualified consulting firm that is right for you:

Look for These Strengths:

- A knowledge of *and* experience with the BPR process *in your industry*.
- An understanding of your business and marketplace.
- A track record for real innovation (not just for recycling or relabeling old ideas).
- A flexible approach that ensures tailoring BPR to your unique situation.
- The diversity and depth of staff experience in all the cross-functional disciplines involved in BPR. The wider the variety of resources available to you, the better.
- The willingness/ability to commit their senior consultants to work with your top managers on this high-level project.
- A wide variety of effective BPR tools and techniques to apply, and experience in using them.
- Experience in team-building and BPR project management.
- International experience, if you have—or may want—an international market operation.
- Sensitivity to the effects dramatic change will have on your managers and workforce.
- Expertise in both BPR and information systems re-engineering.

Watch Out for Consultants Who:

- Use BPR as an excuse to sell you information technology services or equipment.
- Have skills only for part of the job.
- Offer pre-fab solutions to meet your individual needs.
- Are established in other disciplines but who are new to BPR (and who want to use your company to build their capabilities).
- Emphasize their association with well-known academics or workshop leaders. It is unlikely that these busy celebrities will actually work with you.

FIGURE 5-2

SKILL SET FOR EFFECTIVE
TECHNOLOGY-RICH BPR

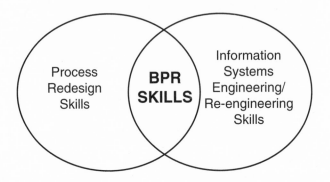

expert in process redesign, the other in systems re-engineering. Often, however, these two sets of experts do not even speak each others' language, much less share the same concepts and approaches. If you have to use more than one outside firm, make sure they have worked together (successfully) on other projects like yours. Otherwise, you'll have the hassle of getting them to cooperate and coordinate—when you hired them to solve, not create, problems.

Know the People You Will Work With

A consulting firm's methodologies and reputation are important, but what you are really paying for is the expertise of the specific people who will work for you. When choosing a consulting firm, it is always advisable to examine the credentials of the *individuals who will work on your project.* Keep the following in mind as you do so:

- Meet the people who will be working directly with

your project. Learn about their individual experience and personal style.

- Ask about their concrete accomplishments. Prior success in project management is an essential indicator of their ability to produce the result you're targeting.

- Talk to others who have worked on BPR projects with the individuals you're considering. Find out about the relationships they developed with their clients. Make sure they delivered what those clients needed to succeed.

In summary, consultants can bring unbiased expertise to your BPR effort and the extra resources you may need to complete its tasks. But they are only an asset if you pick the right firm and the right people. It may be a tough choice, since BPR is still a new venture for many consulting firms and their clients.

Developing a Permanent BPR Capability

Should an organization build a permanent BPR capability? Coopers & Lybrand thinks so, for reasons that Harvard professor John P. Kotter listed in a *Harvard Business Review* article on leadership: "The business world has become more competitive and more volatile. Faster technological change, greater international competition, the deregulation of markets, overcapacity in capital-intensive industries, an unstable oil cartel, raiders with junk bonds, and the changing demographics of the work force are among the many factors that have contributed to this shift. The net result is that doing what was done yesterday, or doing it 5 percent better, is no longer a formula for success. Major changes are more and more necessary to survive and compete effectively in this new environment."

Because change, and the need to respond effectively to change, has become continuous, some organizations have created what are essentially quasi-permanent BPR offices, such as the Xerox Corporation's Director of Business Process Integration and Business Process Board. At Xerox and other corporate giants, the task of redesigning dozens and even hundreds of transnational business processes will go on for years, so the investment in a formalized core capability in BPR makes sense.

However, many organizations will use BPR much less frequently. For them, we recommend having on board one or several individuals who are schooled in BPR methodology. Someone in the executive suite who understands BPR is probably a major plus. Next would be senior line managers who have applied BPR, or who have experience in setting up JIT-type cycle time reduction efforts or flexible factory operations. Increasingly, CIOs and senior systems managers play a critical role in applying breakthrough-enabling technology, and so they are also good choices for extra training in BPR.

Whether your company uses BPR rarely or often, institutionalizing the ability to create major change gives your company a core competency more valuable than any other. By developing the seven characteristics of breakthrough organizations outlined in Chapter 10, you'll be able to identify new opportunities that changing market conditions create, and you'll know how to put the BPR process to work to exploit them. You'll be able to spot, and correct, the problems external change may create for your company, before they reach crisis proportions.

Summary

- The chief executive and senior managers must take the lead in BPR, which involves high-level decisions only they can make. Company veterans of the redesign process emphasize that executive involvement in, and support for, BPR is critical to its success.

- Successful BPR requires a mix of functional/technical

skills and perspectives. Companies can obtain the skills they need in-house or by working with consultants. The participation of both company personnel and BPR experts can provide the fullest perspective on the range of problems that exist and potential solutions to them.

- BPR needs a company's "best and brightest" talent to envision and champion innovations. People with special skills and experience in creative projects should be involved, regardless of their specialties. One of the ways to exploit this talent effectively is to include such individuals on teams that have the managerial, practical, and technical expertise needed to plan and effect change.

- Effective project management is critical to successful BPR. Project managers must have the authority and credibility to get things done on a company-wide basis; the specific credentials of project managers will vary from company to company. Management skills, a strong management plan, and day-to-day support for BPR efforts are vital to every redesign process.

- Companies rarely create permanent in-house BPR capabilities. But it is always advisable to have executives and department heads on board who are knowledgeable about BPR and capable of recognizing the need for radical process change when it arises. Ultimately, it is important to develop the ability to make major changes whenever they are needed.

CHAPTER 6

INFORMATION TECHNOLOGY: CREATING ADVANTAGE OR PAVING COW PATHS?

CHAPTER HIGHLIGHTS

◆

Major improvements in performance come from
the combined use of information technology *(IT)*
and business process redesign.

◆

Without *IT,* some modern business processes
configurations would not be possible.

◆

Process redesign facilitates the application of *IT.*

◆

IT can be used to facilitate the process of BPR.

◆

In most organizations, groups that handle *IT* and process
redesign are separate and distinct, which causes problems.

◆

Systems re-engineering projects are
prime candidates for BPR.

More Than Just Computers

A few years ago, a military organization decided to pilot test a manufacturing resource planning system (MRP II) in an aircraft engine overhaul shop. These systems use information technology to smoothly regulate the flow of work and materials through industrial processes, saving time and money. Coopers & Lybrand advised the shop that the best way to start such a project is to rationalize and streamline the overhaul process before installing the MRP II system. While doing this, a shop team found 15 changes that would greatly enhance product quality and material availability, significantly shorten cycle time, and reduce costs by over $1 million. These improvements were available without the MRP II system, and later helped speed its installation.

Another military organization installed an MRP II system in a large maintenance operation, but it made no real attempt to improve key work processes—employees and managers insisted on continuing the old way of working. In the end, there was only minor improvement in performance; employees protested that the new information system was hard to use, and the effort was scrapped.

The second example is all too typical of how many organizations approach *IT.* By failing to improve processes while installing new information systems, they "pave the cow paths" of inefficient, outmoded work methods. The result often is simply doing the wrong things faster.

Information Indigestion

The chief cause of "paving the cow paths" is commented on in James Martin's *Information Engineering:* "The first motorcars were called 'horseless carriages' and were the same shape as a carriage without a horse. Much later it became recognized that a car should have a different shape. Similarly, the first radio was called 'wireless telegraphy' without the realiza-

"Now that we've automated, we do the wrong thing faster"

tion that broadcasting would bear no resemblance to telegraphy. Today we talk about the 'paperless office' and 'paperless corporation,' but we build (information) systems with screens and data bases that duplicate the previously existing organization of work."

This is one reason why many organizations today are suffering from a severe case of information indigestion. For the past three decades, they have been applying increasingly sophisticated information technology to increasingly outmoded business processes. The result: diminishing returns on *IT* investments and precious capital down the drain. One of the chief objectives of BPR is to bring *IT* and business processes into a synchronized state capable of maximizing return on investment and delivering breakthroughs in competitive advantage.

Enabling Is One Thing; Transforming Another

One way to use *IT* during BPR is as an *enabler* of process redesign. Another is to use *IT* and process redesign together to *transform* business processes. Both can be useful approaches.

Under the enabling concept, process redesign objectives and plans are established first, then are followed by information system plans designed to support them. Says Coopers & Lybrand's Fred Viskovich, "This is a good approach, the one most BPR methods follow today. It's a step up from when people used to plan an information system to exactly imitate an old process, or to force the process into the system. An example of enabling would be when you want a sales force in the field to have quick access to what's in inventory. You give them laptop PCs with modems so they can tap into a central computer, check stocks, and electronically place customer orders."

However, Viskovich thinks the enabling concept suffers from a critical limitation. He's seen clear evidence that if you start planning for a breakthrough without understanding the full potential of information technology, you're liable to miss the opportunity to radically *transform* a business process.

To illustrate the point, he recounts the story of a leading rental car company that had just finished plans for a new information system to collect data on its vehicles. One of its executives was delighted: "This is great! The only thing better would be to put a computer right in the parking lot." Everyone laughed at the notion except an *IT* expert who quietly said, "We can do that, too, you know." Next time you return a rental car, says Viskovich, look at what the parking lot attendants have in their hands: small computers that link into corporate mainframes.

The story's point is that you need to simultaneously consider both business requirements and the full opportunities offered by modern information technology, says Viskovich. "Executives can't say to their *IT* experts, 'Wait outside until we get through planning this breakthrough, then we'll tell you what we need.' To truly transform a business, you have to create a synergy between process redesign and information technology."

Let's consider three aspects of this synergy: the transforming effect of *IT* on business processes, how process redesign

FIGURE 6-1

THREE WAYS TO THINK
ABOUT INFORMATION TECHNOLOGY *(IT)*
AND PROCESS REDESIGN (PR)

APPROACH	RESULT
Traditional	
IT automates existing processes	Paving cow paths
Enablement	
PR planning followed by *IT* planning	Process breakthrough
BreakPoint BPR	
Business requirements simultaneously considered with *IT* capabilities followed by using *IT* and PR to facilitate each other	Transformational process breakthrough

facilitates systems planning, and how *IT* facilitates the application of BPR.

The Transforming Effect of *IT* on Business Processes

Many business process redesigns are simply not possible without the use of information technology. Here are a few examples of mega-breakthroughs that have or will soon transform the business landscape.

Communicating

A state-sponsored, fiber-optic, computer teleconferencing network has started to digitally link experts in many North Carolina universities and research institutions. Through combined video and graphics images, participants who are physically miles apart hold discussions "face-to-face" while examining and manipulating data and images on computer terminals. North Carolina's motivation for this investment in "information superhighways" is to attract high-tech jobs to the state by providing an ideal information-sharing infrastructure.

Designing

Computer-aided design (CAD) has totally automated drafting and design functions, and also many planning tasks. Linked to computer-aided manufacturing (CAM) systems that manage and operate production, CAD has reduced both time and hand-off errors by collapsing once isolated and independent steps into a synchronous design-to-manufacture process flow. CAD has helped cut concept-to-market time for the Chrysler LH and other cars from five years to three or less. CAM systems have been essential in reducing set-up times from weeks to hours in paper products, plastics, and countless other industries.

Searching for a Cure

Once, the search for new medicines nearly always included a multimillion dollar, hit-or-miss process: hand-screening tens of thousands of chemical and organic substances to find a promising few. The challenge has always been two-fold: find something that works, and find a way to get it into the body's cells.

Some drug companies have abbreviated this search through supercomputer modeling of complex organic molecules found in the body's cells. This helps locate and map their receptor sites, the keyholes to entry for life-saving drugs. Then the researchers use the same modeling method to find the keys: other molecules that fit receptor sites. The result is often a ten-fold reduction in time and cost over the old method.

Retail Selling

Once confined to advanced flight and combat simulators, "virtual reality" systems now promise to revolutionize consumer sales. In one of the first retailing applications of virtual reality, customers "wander" through model kitchens that exist only within a computer. They can reach out and "rearrange" appliances and fixtures at will, creating a custom kitchen design in an hour. The system generates precise plans that are sent directly to kitchen installation contractors, along with detailed equipment and materials lists. Virtual reality systems also are expected to have a major impact on processes such as product design, home and commercial construction, and work skills training.

In each of these examples, *IT* was the key to major break-throughs. Yet none of the breakthroughs would have happened unless *IT*'s capabilities were considered at the start of the search for improvement. It is important to remember this during the earliest stages of BPR.

How Process Redesign Facilitates Information Systems Planning

Introducing a major new information system is never easy. The following example shows the two benefits of using process redesign during systems planning:

- Information engineering becomes simpler since redesigning a process often simplifies it.

- Redesigning an operation, including its paper forms

and work procedures, results in a better "fit" between a process and a new information system.

Doing Process Redesign
Well in Advance of a New Information System

Coopers & Lybrand recently worked with one of the nation's largest financial institutions to plan a corporate-wide re-engineered information system. Like many such efforts, the system will be introduced in phases; some business units will come on line before others.

Coopers & Lybrand's consultants included information engineers and process redesign specialists. Cliff Cooksey, one of the redesigners, led a team of clients and consultants who worked on a business process that annually buys and sells a billion dollars in securities. This process was not scheduled to receive the new information system for at least two years.

"The process had many manual operations that could definitely be re-engineered to exploit the full potential of information technology," says Cooksey. "The question was, should every one of those operations be included in the new system? What about unneeded work steps, unread reports, redundancies, rework, expediting, and so on, which add time and money, but not value, to the final products? So our work was aimed at streamlining the process before completing the planning and installation of the information system."

The team found that many manual work steps could be collapsed by the new information system. But there were also new steps needed to feed information into the redesigned business process. Identifying these allowed the team to do better redesigning of all the parts of the "to-be" model. And it alerted the information engineers to potential problems that might not emerge until after the new system started up.

Says Cooksey, "For example, the system might have left out critical links from other business processes to this one. These could be a costly mistake that might slow down this process, and that means money lost in the fast-paced markets it serves. Second, it is much more expensive to go back and fix a problem in an information system, than to prevent it from happening.

"There are nontechnical benefits, too. Our client does not have to wait until the system is up and running to start benefiting from the changes Coopers & Lybrand recommended. Many redesign changes can be made now since they do not depend on the system.

"Also, we now know what the new process probably will look like, in terms of people and how they relate, resource requirements, and interface with other processes," concludes Cooksey. "This means our client can begin the organizational and human change management work needed to make a smooth transition from the 'as-is' to the 'to-be' process, well before installing the information system."

How *IT* Facilitates Process Redesign

Information technology can play a key role in BPR projects through process modeling and electronic group decision-making methods.

Process Modeling

Process modeling software is a major tool in advanced applications of BPR. It allows you to test different process configurations under a variety of assumptions, which speeds process redesign and reduces the risk of errors.

For example, Cliff Cooksey's team began its analysis of the securities operation by using Coopers & Lybrand's SPARKS computerized process simulation system to map out a model of the "as-is" business process. This involved gathering data for the model by interviewing process personnel, reviewing procedures manuals, looking at performance results, and constructing work flow diagrams.

This model helped the team look for immediate and future

process improvement and redesign opportunities. Next, SPARKS technology allowed them to simulate alternative future scenarios for the process. These included significant changes in manual labor, responsibilities, and tasks. The resulting "to-be" process model was ideal for information systems planning.

"In the future, I think we will be able to go a step further than SPARKS," says Fred Viskovich. "What everyone wants is a software package that combines both process data and technical systems modeling. Some folks say they've invented the package, but that's really not true. But when it happens, you'll see a great acceleration and improvement in BPR."

Group Decision-Making

One of the very tough problems in BPR is to get groups of people to develop fresh ideas and then agree on them. Anyone who has suffered through countless long meetings that produced neither result knows how difficult this can be.

Electronic group decision-making systems are specifically designed to allow large groups to quickly isolate and describe issues, generate ideas, and agree on the complex issues involved in radical change. They range from portable polling systems that use palm-sized numeric keypads to record, aggregate, and feed back the opinions of a group to sophisticated electronic "decision rooms" with computer terminals at every seat.

Systems like these have vastly cut the time needed for important decisions, which is why they are an important tool in Coopers & Lybrand's fast-paced BreakPoint BPR methodology. For example, *Computerworld* reports that Boeing saved 1,773 calendar days in 64 meetings over a nine-month period by using an electronic group decision-making system. Also, these systems keep all opinions anonymous, and so encourage an honesty often lacking in traditional meetings.

But saving time and promoting candor are not the only benefits, according to a team of U.S. and Canadian researchers led by R. Brent Gallupe. Their research, reported in the

Academy of Management Journal, consisted of a controlled experiment comparing the results of small and large groups using electronic and nonelectronic (i.e., verbal) brainstorming to generate new ideas. The result: with the electronic approach, the larger groups generated more unique ideas and more high-quality ideas, and reported they were more satisfied than when they used verbal brainstorming.

Speaking of group decision-making, let's look at two groups in most organizations that need to do a better job of communicating if they want transformational breakthroughs.

Strategy and Leadership:
Bringing *IT* and Process Redesign Together

In most organizations, the groups that handle process redesign and information systems re-engineering are distinct. Often, they rarely talk with each other, much less cooperate. As this chapter should make clear, that needs to change. Only by merging the skills of both groups can an organization hope to maximize returns from BPR investments.

This does not have to be a physical merger (although some predict that such a merger is inevitable). It can be achieved by:

- Simultaneous consideration of both business require-ments and the potential of information technology.

- Developing a corporate-wide strategic plan for gaining and sustaining competitive advantage.

- Creating a "business architecture," a model based on the strategic plan that shows the desired "to-be" config-uration of an organization's processes.

- Using that business architecture to guide development of an "information systems architecture," a model that includes hardware, software, communications, and user interface.

- Requiring that process redesign specialists, information engineers, line managers, and employees team up to implement both business and systems architectures.

Making this happen is a job for executives—in other words, it requires leadership from the top. This has to be strong, ongoing leadership since both the redesign and the information system groups may be tempted to return to old patterns of noncooperation.

Finally, executives will need to spot opportunities to apply combined process redesign solutions/*IT* solutions to their businesses, such as the major systems re-engineering projects scheduled for the next few years.

Systems Re-Engineering Opportunities in the 1990s

Have American organizations learned their lesson about paving cow paths yet? If not, they'd better learn soon, or we're going to waste a whole lot of money. In 1992, U.S. organizations will spend nearly $18 billion re-engineering their information systems, according to G2 Research, Inc., in a report commissioned by Coopers & Lybrand. This investment will increase to $40 billion by 1997, with the lion's share going for new hardware; converting old computer codes into newer, more powerful and flexible languages; and ensuring better communication among different hardware configurations.

This *may* establish a better *IT* infrastructure in America—but then again, maybe not. Many organizations will not change their business processes along with their information systems, and some will even persist in automating processes that outlived their very purpose long ago. "That's putting whipped cream on garbage," said Coopers & Lybrand's William Wheeler in a recent *Fortune* article on U.S. productivity.

What a terrible waste, both for a company and for

FIGURE 6-2

STRATEGY & LEADERSHIP FROM THE TOP ARE NECESSARY TO COORDINATE PROCESS REDESIGN AND SYSTEMS ENGINEERING

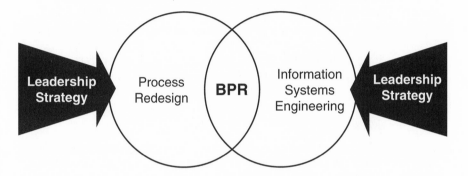

America! We cannot afford this waste in today's competitive environment. Information technology can be our greatest asset in this competition—we are the best in the world at using it. But this asset can turn into a liability without business process redesign.

Therefore, every systems re-engineering project is a candidate for parallel process improvement through redesign. Otherwise, America's economic epitaph will read: "They were great at paving cow paths."

Summary

- Information technology and business processes often are out of sync. *IT* has developed much faster than process improvement, which has led to the application of modern technology to outmoded business processes. The result is "doing the wrong things faster."

- Thinking of *IT* as an "enabler" of process redesign is a good approach and will lead to breakthroughs. But transformational thinking—simultaneously considering business requirements and *IT* capabilities—is better because it reveals new opportunities.

- Doing BPR in advance of installing new information systems makes the *IT* effort easier by rationalizing and streamlining operations before they are automated.

- Computerized process modeling and electronic group decision-making systems speed and improve the conduct of BPR.

- Most organizations have separate units for process redesign and *IT*. This can cause major communication and coordination problems. They need to act as a team, but only corporate-wide strategy and leadership from the top will make this happen.

- It makes no sense to conduct a systems re-engineering project without using process redesign. To do otherwise leads to automating processes that should be improved (and perhaps even eliminated).

CHAPTER 7

CHANGE MANAGEMENT

CHAPTER HIGHLIGHTS

Often, the most difficult problems in BPR
come from human and cultural issues, not technology.
Change management helps to align people and culture
with the changes brought about by BPR.

Leadership is the most critical factor in
change management; without it, expect failure.

Change management involves a series of steps that,
if taken correctly, will foster acceptance of BPR changes.

Resistance to change can be overcome
by careful planning and action.

Displacement of employees during BPR can be
dealt with in a variety of creative ways.

♦

An organization sometimes must change its culture
in order to ensure the success of
redesigned processes.

Getting Ready for Change:
The Human and Cultural Sides

" **A** breakthrough process often requires changes that go far beyond those made to its technology and work methods," says Lynn Berberich, vice president of human resources at PHH FleetAmerica, a major vehicle fleet management organization. Below, we outline what she means.

Culture. Some of PHH's redesigned processes are being managed by employee work teams. Before, they were run by a typical hierarchical organizational approach in a culture where supervisors gave orders and employees followed them. In the new team structure, employees have to know how to manage, while supervisors must be team coaches and mentors. Says Berberich, "Those are major changes in culture, and they do not happen automatically. We have to provide training, motivation, and positive feedback to help people learn and adopt these new skills."

Skills mix. Other skills are important, too. PHH's new information systems require technical skills that people whose work is paper-based never had the opportunity to learn. And the new team structure puts a premium on inter-personal communication skills, as does increased contact between clients and employees. According to Berberich, "Our challenge has been to retrain as many of our current employees as we can in these skills, and hire new people with them."

Displacement. The new information system produces a lot less paper, so PHH needs fewer people to handle it. PHH has planned for this, as can be seen in Figure 7-1, PHH's "Employment Action Matrix." It shows PHH's determination to provide displaced employees with the best opportunities the company can afford to give them.

Communication. Major change can be frightening; an essential way to dispel the fear is through communication. One way PHH does this is through a high-quality monthly newslet-

FIGURE 7-1

PHH FLEETAMERICA
EMPLOYMENT ACTION MATRIX

Objective: To be a flexible and broadly trained organization capable of redeploying employees affected by strategic and operational changes with a minimum of service, climate, and career disruptions

"Future Skills" Possessed by the Employee	Job Availability	Employment Action
High transferability	Appropriate *or*	→ Offer transfer (may be promotion, lateral, or demotion)
	No regular job open	→ Offer temporary or project assignment → Offer assignment to business process re-engineering team
Limited/no transferability but high trainability	Anticipated future needs *or*	→ Train to future specifications
	Career opportunities exist in outsourced or network partner organization	→ Facilitate move to new organization
Limited/no transferability	Critical work in progress	→ Stay incentive with career transition benefits at conclusion
	or No anticipated internal or partner opportunities	→ Termination with career transition benefits and outplacement
Performance problems	N/A	→ Aggressively manage to success, to demotion, or to termination

ter, *The BPR Report.* Besides pointing out the benefits of what will come from redesigned processes, the newsletter deals frankly with issues such as displacement. Other methods of communication at PHH include regular meetings to discuss BPR and its changes, and making extensive use of teams in planning and carrying out the BPR effort.

Readiness for change. Before starting its BPR projects, PHH needed to know how well people in the targeted processes were prepared for change. Top management learned this through an organizational impact assessment, the results of which are shown in Figure 7-2. Such assessments determine the capability of an organization as a whole, or groups within it, to make major changes. "The assessment showed us that we had to shore up some of the readiness factors in each process," said Berberich. "Doing this was as important as any of the technical measures we made in process redesign. However, the job was easier because our leaders were ready—and leadership is where change begins."

Change Management

What Lynn Berberich and PHH are doing is called *change management:* the process of aligning an organization's people and culture with changes in business strategy, structure and systems. Change management is as much a part of BreakPoint BPR strategy as process redesign and information technology. We feel this is necessary to overcome resistance to change, and to ensure that the individual changes people make as a result of BPR move in the desired direction.

Change Leadership

Change management is equal parts leadership and management of planned change. The leadership part of it determines the direction of change through strategic planning and goal setting. Leaders communicate this direction through personal contact with managers and employees and through other means

FIGURE 7-2

ORGANIZATIONAL IMPACT
ASSESSMENT, PHH FLEETAMERICA

Organization Readiness in:

	Process A	Process B	Process C
Leadership			
– stakeholder	+	✓	+
– management	+	✓	✓
Change management/ self-confidence	- / ✓	- / ✓	- / ✓
Understanding/ commitment	-	- / ✓	- / ✓
Talent available	-	- / ✓	✓
Sense of urgency	✓	✓	- / ✓

- Not ready   ✓ OK   + Very ready

such as clear-cut objectives. They marshall the resources needed for change, including recruiting an organization's "best and brightest" managers to carry out the change process. Leaders closely monitor the progress of change, and are ready to lend a hand when obstacles are encountered. Good leaders take great pains to recognize and reward the accomplishments of BPR project managers and the success of all personnel in making change happen.

Leadership also means leaders play an active role in the change process and model the new behaviors required for the success of redesigned processes. As noted in the PHH example above, such leadership is absolutely essential in BPR.

Management of Planned Change

The management of planned change consists of coordinating and carrying out the various steps in the change process. These are listed below, in approximate order of their occurrence.

Describe the change. This involves writing a good description of both the "as-is" process before it is changed and the "to-be" process, after BPR. You will find it helpful to involve in this exercise those who will be affected by the change. Involving these workers will promote their "buying into" the change, and also will provide insights you may have overlooked.

Identify the forces for and against the change. Follow these descriptions with a review of the types and degrees of support and resistance you can expect for the change. Figure 7-3 shows how to do this analysis. On the left side of the chart, list the various forces for the change, such as committed leadership, sense of urgency in the organization, availability of funding, or technological capabilities. On the right, list the forces against change, such as fear of layoffs, a history of failed attempts to change, resistance from labor, and so on. Then rank the forces on each side of the chart in order of their potential impact on the change. Before and during BPR, you will have to overcome the forces against change (or at least neutralize them), while reinforcing the forces for change.

Force field analysis will prove useful throughout BPR planning and redesign, so use it often. It can be applied to an entire process redesign effort or to parts of the effort, such as changing individual behaviors, which we discuss next.

Determine the individual and group actions that will support the planned change. This starts by listing the individual actions needed to successfully do a job in the redesigned process. These actions may include reading manuals, perform-

FIGURE 7-3

FORCE FIELD ANALYSIS

FORCES FOR:	FORCES AGAINST:
Top leader support	Some middle management resistance
Recent loss of work to private contractors	Complacency among units
Strategic plan	Fear of job loss if productivity increases
	Failure of previous productivity effort
	Plans tend to sit on shelves

1) Describe the issue/problem.
2) Develop an "ideal" solution.
3) Brainstorm to get a list of forces for and forces against the solution.
4) Rank the forces in order of their importance or effect.
5) Develop change management strategy for removing the most important forces against, and for reinforcing the forces for.

ing calculations, operating a machine, answering customer questions, and so on. Your personnel (or human resources) department can be very helpful in making this list.

List the behaviors that will support the actions. These may be different from current behaviors. For example, in some redesigned processes, you will want to see increased teamwork, more risk-taking, cross-functional cooperation, employee involvement, and willingness to learn. Knowing this in advance can help you plan for changes in work structures, reward systems, and other factors that affect such behaviors.

Make an honest assessment of readiness for change. How ready are your personnel to accept the changes you propose? If they understand the urgency for change, and trust both management's and their own ability to create change, they are ready for it. If personnel see no need for change and feel they are not valued by management, then expect major resistance.

There are many ways to conduct such an assessment, including surveys or focus groups of employees and managers; reviews of complaints, grievances, and exit interviews; and honest and open discussions with employees. If you find there will be barriers to change, you have to deal with them before or during the introduction of a redesigned process (see box).

Define new behaviors. Be explicit. Provide clear examples of the new behaviors, rather than general descriptions of them. Involve managers and employees in fleshing out your definitions. Look for positive role models among managers and employees in your organization. Finally, *be* a role model for the new behavior—unless *you* practice it, no one else will.

Remove barriers. Barriers may include rules and regulations that cause needless work or delay, or otherwise prevent people from doing work under the new process.

Train, train, train. Provide training in the work skills and behavioral skills you want to promote. This needs to be a continuous effort since new people will enter the redesigned process throughout its life cycle.

The Organizational Assessment Process

One way to assess the readiness to change in your organization is through a cultural climate survey, such as Coopers & Lybrand's Organizational Assessment Process (OAP). The OAP's core is a survey that records individual responses to questions about the degree of control people feel they have over their jobs, their willingness to change, their job satisfaction, how much they trust management, and other factors that can determine the success of a major change effort.

Results from an OAP survey are benchmarked or compared to those in a data base of 300,000 other survey participants from 150+ organizations in the U.S. and overseas. Many of these organizations have been thoroughly analyzed on their financial and market performance, and comparisons can be limited to those that are "best-in-class" for their industries. Results also can be compared by job classification, such as engineers or managers. These comparisons provide a "benchmark" of the readiness of your organization and individual employees.

OAP results can be used to target those work units most willing to accept change. OAP results also can be used to identify problems that must be addressed before change can be introduced. Our clients often do this by forming teams from within targeted work units to find solutions to the problems OAP identifies.

Reward desired behavior and create disincentives for undesired behavior. This often involves the complete restructuring of performance measurement and reward systems. More specifically, it means taking the time to find and spotlight persons and events that personify the new way of doing things.

Involve the groups targeted for behavior change in the process of creating the change. Have them develop plans for supporting the change, then support their plans to make the change. Involving middle managers is extremely important since they are the critical link between executive desires for change and employees' ability and willingness to make change happen.

Monitor the progress of change. If you're scheduling training and orientations, or trying to encourage employee involvement in certain processes, this step includes making sure that: teams are being formed, managers are delegating authority to line employees, and people are taking advantage of the new training programs.

Maintain an active communication program. Use newsletters, video tapes, meetings, and other methods to inform personnel about plans and progress.

By taking these steps, you ensure that change will happen, and that it will be directed toward the objectives you have targeted. However, you also must deal—to a greater or lesser extent, depending on the magnitude of process redesign—with resistance to change.

Overcoming Resistance to Change

It is wise to expect at least some resistance to the changes brought about by BPR. In some cases, this resistance is quite rational: some people are going to lose power, opportunity for advancement, and perhaps even their jobs. Other people will simply resist being made to change—they want to have a voice in how they do their work. Finally, everyone is at least a little afraid of change because it represents risk.

Fortunately, there are a number of methods and techniques that will help to overcome this resistance among individuals and small groups.

Communication Is Important

Rumors abound during any major transition. Besides causing needless and often paralyzing fears, rumors can be real time wasters—people discuss them instead of doing real work. Rumors also have a way of reaching customers and suppliers,

Reasons People Resist Change	Actions to Address Resistance
When change comes from without, people often feel a loss of control of their lives and the things that they value.	Seek every opportunity to involve people who will be affected by a change. Use teams of process managers and employees throughout the BreakPoint BPR process.
Excessive uncertainty about the personal impact of the change.	Provide as much information as possible about the change itself and how it will affect individual workers. This means letting people know the bad news as well as the good. Even when the news is bad, knowing what to expect can be less stressful than uncertainty.
The magnitude of the change seems enormous.	Make change manageable by the individual. This includes providing the opportunity to experiment with the new way in a non-threatening environment. Also, it may mean phasing in change over time.
Loss of face because the old ways suddenly seem "bad."	Discuss the old process in a positive light; honor its successes and those who made these victories possible. Never, ever ridicule the old method—this will make people feel stupid and they will resent you for it.
Concerns about future competence.	Supply adequate training in the new methods: formal training with subsequent feedback on performance.
Change has ripple effects that may not be immediately obvious.	Make the new process design flexible enough to deal with these effects. Also, reward those who point out the new problems, and involve them in resolving them.

which can cause canceled orders or loss of credit. These are
even more reasons for management to be open and honest about
its plans for BPR and any major displacements the change will
generate.

Top management in many organizations take rumor control seriously and use forums, newsletters, memos, and special
phone centers to answer employee questions. Doing this well in
advance of a major change alleviates fear of the unknown, so
that people can get on with their lives (and the company's work).

It's even possible to be creative about communicating by
using humor to squelch a rumor. While consolidating 11 work
units into a "flexible factory" for processing financial documents, the Bank of Boston faced serious morale problems due
to rumors circulating among employees. Management invited
all affected personnel to a meeting at a movie theater rented for
this purpose. As the employees sat waiting for the meeting to
start, the Marvin Gaye song "Heard it Through the Grapevine"
began playing. Down the aisle and up onto the stage danced top
executives of the bank, dressed in "California Raisin" costumes.
During the meeting, each executive stood up (in costume) to
give employees the facts—and not all the news was good. But
imitating the popular television commercial for raisins was a
good laugh for everyone, and helped defuse a tense situation.

Before dismissing this example as undignified, think about
the fact that it worked. Even more, the meeting was a signal to
all managers to be open and honest, and to listen to employees.

Dealing with Displacement

Layoffs are sometimes the by-product of process redesign.
Often, those who remain face equally serious psychological
problems, which some have called "survival guilt." Also, the
"survivors" face practical problems in adjusting to redesigned
jobs. Thus, an organization has two sets of responsibilities
when layoffs happen: for those who have to go and those that
remain.

Those Who Have To Go

At the start of this chapter, we showed how PHH FleetAmerica planned for the displacement of some of its personnel during BPR. Here, we outline how organizations throughout the country have developed creative ways to aid personnel whose jobs have been eliminated. These include:

- Special efforts to retrain them for new positions in the organization;

- Temporary consulting arrangements with some of the displaced employees;

- Attractive early retirement packages;

- Large severance payments based on length of employment;

- Continuation of benefits such as life and health insurance for extended periods after separation; and

- Extensive personal and family counseling.

We will now discuss three other methods in detail that are relatively new to corporate and government employers.

Outplacement. Often, organizations contract with a professional outplacement firm to provide guidance and assistance to all laid-off personnel. This outplacement assistance includes guidance counseling, personal counseling, help in preparing resumes, providing office space and secretarial support, and holding regular support group meetings.

Once, this was done only for top managers and executives. Today, corporations such as IBM make it part of the separation benefits for all employees through professional outplacement firms. Besides meeting its responsibilities to loyal employees who must leave, an organization that hires a reputable outplacement firm ensures that its people will be helped by experienced professionals.

Temporary labor pools. These arrangements provide a means of retaining displaced employees until new jobs open up. For example, Coopers & Lybrand assisted several large military industrial organizations in reducing the amount of work needed for indirect or overhead functions such as personnel and administration. About 450 employees were displaced as part of a large process improvement project at the Norfolk, Virginia, Navy Public Works Center. Coopers & Lybrand worked with the center to establish a temporary labor pool where displaced employees could be sent for up to one year. During that year, labor pool personnel were assigned temporary jobs throughout the center as the need arose. As new permanent jobs opened up, members of the labor pool were given preference for them. Also, all received outplacement counseling and assistance. By the end of the year, all but a handful of the employees had found jobs in the center or in the community.

Outsourcing that includes former employees. Outsourcing is the practice of contracting out for services once run by an organization's employees and managers. Part of PHH FleetAmerica's redesign strategy was to outsource some of its non-core functions, such as the operation of its computer center. To minimize job loss by its internal operators, PHH required that the contractor give former employees preference in staffing the new arrangement. Many were hired and continue to work within the walls of PHH. The added benefit to these employees is more potential for advancement since computer center operation is a core function of the contractor.

Admittedly, some of these solutions add up to sizable short-term costs for an organization. The payoff comes from less resistance to change during the transition process, and a more loyal workforce after BPR. Finally, communities and the government look favorably on employers that take responsibility for the transitions created by layoffs.

Those Who Remain

Employees who remain after a large layoff often face both psychological and practical problems. Unless you deal with these, expect major problems in running newly redesigned processes.

Psychological. In the *Academy of Management Executive,* researchers Kim Cameron, Sarah Freeman, and Aneil Mishra of the University of Michigan examined the psychological effects of large layoffs on remaining employees in 30 automotive companies. They found that the workers experienced "survivor guilt," manifested as ". . . increased anxiety about job loss, decreased loyalty to the firm, and guilt feelings regarding displaced co-workers. Survivor guilt occurs when the remaining employees feel guilty about working overtime, for example, or receiving paychecks when their friends and former co-workers may not be working at all. [The survivors feel that] the attributes traditionally valued in good employees—loyalty, hard work, and personal competence—no longer count in the firm. Individuals who displayed these traits still lost their jobs."

The researchers found several factors among companies that were successful in helping survivors to deal with these psychological problems:

- Management made special efforts to communicate the rationale and circumstances underlying the layoffs, efforts characterized by openness and a willingness to listen to employee complaints and suggestions. This included posting the latest information on bulletin boards, and formal and informal forums for employees and managers to discuss the issues;

- Management reaffirmed the value it placed on the remaining employees, and assured them that neither they nor the displaced workers were to blame for the circumstances that caused the layoffs;

- Employees slated to remain were included in the front-end of planning for new operations; and

- The organizations held special events to mark the end of the "old era" and the beginning of the new.

Finally, people at all levels understand the reason an organization is in business: to serve customers. Layoffs are more palatable to those who remain if they can clearly see the link between redesigned processes and improved products and customer service.

Practical. Whether due to layoffs or job redesign, some personnel face severe practical problems in making the adjustment to a smaller workforce or a new way of working:

- Some personnel find that they have a suddenly increased workload. According to the Michigan researchers, "Management survivors were required to manage a larger number of employees, maintain accountability for multiple (often new) functions, and to coordinate among more subunits than before. Management burn-out was a common complaint." In BPR, personnel usually are required to learn new ways of working and new responsibilities, both of which can be extremely demanding on their time.

- In some organizations that have had large layoffs, the typical practice is for more senior personnel to take over the jobs of junior people, who in turn displace others, and so on down the line. This seniority "bumping" creates a costly and often demoralizing ripple effect throughout an organization. Often, the senior personnel are not as qualified for the new positions as those they displaced.

The solutions to these problems include:

- Providing personnel targeted for redesigned jobs with ample time for training and development before they assume new responsibilities;

- Listening to the complaints and suggestions of personnel once they start in their new positions and making adjustments to their workload, training, and development;

- To prevent "bumping," systems such as the previously mentioned temporary employment pool provide a place for senior employees to wait for jobs more in keeping with their experience and skills;

- Some organizations use qualifying tests for new positions that senior personnel must take before "bumping" junior personnel; and

- Many organizations offer incentives such as cash awards and step promotions for people who take advantage of training and development activities.

What we have discussed so far in this chapter relates to aligning individuals and groups with redesigned business processes. Often, however, for these processes to function effectively, you need to realign your organization's entire culture.

Realigning Organizational Culture

Just like the tribes of old, every organization has a unique culture. This culture is defined by a set of official and unofficial norms, values, and beliefs that regulate both the positive and negative behaviors of managers and employees. These are not abstract concepts, but rather models and lessons everyone has to learn in order to prosper, or at least survive, in a modern organization.

For example, most organizations will find that their culture inhibits employee involvement in introducing change. In an article in *Incentive*, Coopers & Lybrand's Cliff Cooksey and Allied-Signal's Donnee Ramelli reported that the average North American suggestion program rejects two out of three employee ideas, according to data submitted by 289 member organizations of the National Association of Suggestion Systems (NASS). Thus, the American management *norm* is to spurn employee ideas.

It should come as no surprise, then, that employee *beliefs* about suggestion programs can be summed up as "Why try?" In fact, NASS figures show that only 12 formal suggestions were made per 100 workers in 1989. That finding is echoed in a 1992 report on factory employee focus groups conducted by the National Association of Manufacturers: "Worker groups felt that they knew the most and could contribute but were almost never asked. They had either no experience with suggestion programs, or no faith that they would be rewarded for their good ideas." In short, the average American organization's *culture* is one that does not *value* employee ideas.

This is a problem for organizations that want to see more employee involvement in controlling and improving processes once they are redesigned. To promote more involvement, such organizations will need to change their norms and values. This might include retraining and motivating managers to seek out and accept employee ideas, monitoring managers' performance in this area, and developing better manager and employee reward systems that promote suggestion making. Training, monitoring, and rewarding are specific, concrete actions with measurable results—they are variables management can use to change culture.

Other culturally determined behaviors that are critical to the success of major changes include:

Teamwork. Consider the reward structure for teamwork versus individual effort. In most organizations, particularly those chasing the chimera of "pay-for-performance," individual

FIGURE 7-4

SELECTED VARIABLES
THAT CAN BE MANIPULATED TO ALTER
ORGANIZATIONAL CULTURE

Reward Systems	Promotions, salaries, bonuses, performance appraisal
Organizational Structure	Rigid to flexible, individual to team
Customer Contact	Opportunity to talk with internal/external customers or observe them using a process' output
Employee Input	Enhanced team or individual idea/suggestion programs, monitoring managers' results in promoting employee ideas
Performance Feedback	Information systems that give personnel quick feedback on their process' performance in meeting customer/management requirements
Learning	Training for job, process improvement, and basic reading/math skills; support participation in trade & professional groups; pay for outside education for managers and employees
Decision Making	Train managers & employees in and require use of fact-based decision tools and procedures
Job Scope	Broaden job descriptions & work responsibilities, cross-train in different skills needed in a process

productivity bonuses are the norm. By contrast, companies such as General Foods, which makes heavy use of self-managed work teams, reward team rather than individual productivity. Still other companies stress individual contributions to multi-skill work teams by providing extra pay for people who cross-train in several skills. These rewards reinforce desirable teamwork behavior.

Cooperation across organizational boundaries. Since business processes usually are cross-functional, they require cooperation among departments, divisions, field offices, and other work units. However, the "chain-of-command" norm of most organizations impedes cooperation in problem-solving at the lower echelons, while inter-unit rivalries prevent it at the top. In such organizations, cooperation is the exception, not the norm. Allied-Signal, a Coopers & Lybrand client, is changing to a culture of cooperation by creating "molecules" of managers and employees from many departments who work on cross-functional projects and problem-solving.

Independent decision-making. Traditionally, managers make virtually all of the decisions required to run a business. In many cases, an organization's culture makes it clear that employees *do not* make decisions. However, after a process redesign, employees may be given considerable leeway in making decisions, often while in direct contact with customers. Computerized decision rules and artificial intelligence systems may help them make decisions, but in ambiguous situations these employees will have to use their own judgment. Their guidance will have to come from the norms, beliefs, and values that embody the principles considered most important to an organization's success. This is one reason that major corporations and units of government spend so much time identifying their corporate values: these are the touchstones employees and managers use to determine "the right thing to do."

What is the best culture for an organization? The answer varies according to the nature of its processes, products, market, customers, workforce demographics, and local economy and customs. There is no universal prescription for organizational culture, except this: know what yours is, and if necessary change it to promote competitive advantage.

Breakthrough Culture for Breakthrough Change

If and when you decide to make a breakthrough change, consider the seven characteristics of an organization capable of producing breakthroughs on demand. Outlined in Chapter 10, these include the values, norms, and beliefs of an organizational culture that is ready for major change.

Is an organization's culture set in stone? Hardly, as evidenced by the actions mentioned in this chapter that some organizations have taken to change their cultures. As for promoting more employee suggestions, ask the Milliken Corporation, winner of the Malcolm Baldrige National Quality Award. A few years ago, Milliken had a typical suggestion program, with run-of-the-mill results. Now, Milliken accepts nearly all employee ideas. In 1991, it received *2,200 suggestions per 100 employees.*

In a culture like Milliken's, you can be sure that people are ready to accept breakthrough change. Why? Twenty-two times a year, the average Milliken employee makes change happen.

Summary

- You can design technically advanced processes *but . . .*

  if your organization's human resources and systems are not aligned to support the process and . . .

  if your work culture does not reinforce risk taking, learning, and innovation . . .

  genuine, sustained, successful change will not happen. In fact, most success in achieving radical change comes from correctly handling the human factors.

- Change management is the process of aligning an organization's people and culture with changes in business strategy, structure, and systems. It is essential to plan for change management during the initial stages of BPR, and to use its methods throughout redesign and implementation.

- Dealing with displaced personnel is an important part of BPR change management. Not only is this your responsibility to loyal employees who must leave the organization, it helps allay the fears of those who remain.

- Wise executives treat their organization's culture as a variable, and change it to meet new circumstances.

CHAPTER 8

BPR AND CONTINUOUS IMPROVEMENT: CHOOSE BOTH, USE BOTH

CHAPTER HIGHLIGHTS

◆

Combining BPR and continuous improvement
in your redesign strategy provides both immediate
and long-term gains.

◆

Some TQM continuous
improvement procedures, ranging from teamwork to
advanced problem solving, can be used to help
redesign a business process.

◆

BPR offers an excellent opportunity to introduce
TQM as an ongoing way of doing business.

C ontinuous improvement goes by many names: kaizen, total quality management, total quality control, total quality, zero defects, and quality circles. But it means just one thing: involving everyone—managers, employees, customers, suppliers—in a relentless, scientific and customer-focused pursuit of improvement of business processes. TQM methods used during the BPR process can be used afterwards to sustain and increase gains.

Using TQM Methods during a Breakthrough

In 1986, AT&T was ready to close its Louisiana business telephone system factory, the Shreveport Works. Off-shore factories in Asia built these systems faster and cheaper, and several of Shreveport's product lines had been sent overseas for manufacture. Already, over a thousand workers had lost their jobs because of this trend.

AT&T was willing to give Shreveport one more chance, and the factory's managers and employees rallied to the challenge. Working with Coopers & Lybrand, within a few months they completely redesigned their entire production process to reflect just-in-time (JIT) cycle time reduction principles. JIT was selected because it accelerates operations, makes short production runs economical, and reduces in-process and finished goods inventory. At the same time, factory managers asked Coopers & Lybrand to help introduce TQM as the overall operating approach at Shreveport.

During the JIT redesign, the factory encountered a major technical barrier to success: the wave-soldering process, used in making printed circuit boards. Nearly all products went through this process, but up to 40 percent of them came out with defects. New equipment was not the answer since the wave-soldering machine was state-of-the-art.

TQM breakthrough. A team of engineers and employees tackled the problem with a TQM tool called design of experiments (specifically, Taguchi methods). This methodology enabled them to examine the many potential reasons for the defects, experiment with solutions, and isolate the chief culprit, called "solder theft." Adding outside vendors who supplied components that were processed by the wave-soldering machine to the team (also a TQM practice), the Shreveport engineers and workers redesigned the components. This, with a few other experimental changes, solved the problem. Shreveport's wave-soldering process became the *only one in the world that was practically defect-free.* That's competitive advantage.

Results. Solving the problem saved $15 million in scrap and rework costs—many times more than the expense of introducing JIT and TQM. But the real gain was in time. Before, wave soldering was a major bottleneck; now, work flowed through it quickly and smoothly. Within a year, Shreveport took back the product lines it had lost to overseas factories. Today, the factory ships those products to the same Asian countries that used to make them for AT&T.

Shreveport continues to use TQM as an ongoing improvement strategy in both production and support processes, so it constantly improves on the gains made in its original breakthrough. In this chapter, we will see how organizations use both BPR and continuous improvement to jump ahead, and stay ahead of the competition.

What Is Continuous Improvement?

Most people think of continuous improvement as small teams of employees who routinely enhance the operations they work in. However, that is only part of this approach. Actually, continuous improvement has become a code word for a new style of *quality management* built around the goal of raising customer satisfaction through process improvement. *Quality,* as used here, is another code word and stands for the physical quality of products and services, productivity, efficiency, working environment, safety, ethics, corporate responsibility to the community, and every other value of any organization.

In quality management, quality is always defined by customer expectations. Therefore, this approach emphasizes finding out what customers want because *they* are the ultimate judges of whether an organization is doing "the right thing" for them.

Quality management's operational objective is to do the right thing *better*. This means focusing on *process quality*. The reason: if processes are of high quality and do the right thing, the products and services they make will be, too. *Total quality management* is the application of this objective to all processes in an organization, from corporate board room procedures on down.

Principles of TQM

TQM is a practical management philosophy that provides guidance in the everyday decisions of business. The principles it follows are in many ways different from those of traditional management, as shown in Figure 8-1. These principles are practiced daily, as part of the normal way of doing business. Later in this chapter, we will show an example of how they are used in Jacksonville, Florida.

While Shreveport got a "home run" by using TQM on wave soldering, most of the time the improvements gained from this approach are small "base hits." They add up to major gains, however, and are within the grasp of every employee, so that all people in an organization are trained and encouraged to make them happen. This includes managers, who use TQM methods to plan for and coordinate improvement.

Compelling Reasons for Continuous Improvement

Why are these small improvements so important? Here's what can happen to a breakthrough without them.

Performance starts to decay. Call it entropy, the relentless force in physics that pulls every ordered structure into

FIGURE 8-1

COMPARISON OF TRADITIONAL AND
TQM MANAGEMENT PRINCIPLES

Traditional Management	Total Quality Management
Needs of users of products and services defined by specialists	**Customer focus,** where users of products and services define what they want
Errors and waste tolerated if they do not exceed set standards	**No tolerance** for errors, waste, and work that does not add value to products and services
Products and services inspected for problems, then "fixed"	**Prevention** of problems
Many decisions governed by assumptions and gut feelings	**Fact-based decisions** using hard data and scientific procedures
Short-term planning based around budget cycle	**Long-term planning** based on improving mission performance
Product or service designed sequentially by isolated departments	**Simultaneous design** of total product or service life cycle by teams from many functions
Control and improvement by individual managers and specialists	**Teamwork** among managers, specialists, employees, vendors, customers, and partner agencies
Improvement focused on one-time breakthroughs such as computers and automation	**Continuous improvement** of every aspect of how work is done
Vertical structure and centralization based on control	**Horizontal and decentralized structure** based on maximizing value added to products and services
Short-term contracts awarded based on price	**Vendor partnership** of long-term buyer/seller obligations, based on quality and continuous improvement

chaos. It has many causes: people stop using standard procedures, equipment is poorly maintained, management loses interest after a breakthrough, and increased demands strain capacity.
The top chart in Figure 8-2 shows how this affects post-breakthrough performance—after a plateau, things go downhill.

Competitors achieve a new standard of excellence that
makes yours obsolete (in the eyes of customers, at least). This
has the same effect on competitive advantage as the situations
described in the previous paragraph.

Factors change in ways that render your process incapable
of performing as needed. These may include customer requirements, labor costs, energy costs, raw material availability, government regulations, and so on. Effect: same as the previous
two paragraphs.

If any of these things happen, then you have two choices:
either try BPR all over again, or be second-rate. Both are expensive alternatives.

With continuous improvement, you gradually raise performance beyond the original standard of excellence set by the
breakthrough. This means competitors will have to stretch
harder and spend more money to exceed your constantly rising
standard. Also, you use TQM methodologies to adjust the
process to overcome, to the extent possible, factors that render it
less than effective.

The result of this combined BPR/TQM strategy is shown
in the bottom chart in Figure 8-2: breakthroughs followed by
smaller but constant performance increases. This is the performance profile of a world-class breakthrough organization, able
to take advantage of every opportunity—large and small—to
stay ahead of the competition.

Continuous Improvement
after a Breakthrough

BreakPoint BPR always designs in continuous improvement during a BPR project, in order to sustain and improve

FIGURE 8-2

PERFORMANCE AFTER BREAKTHROUGHS

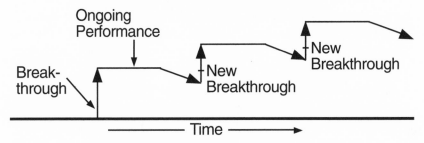

Without Continuous Improvement

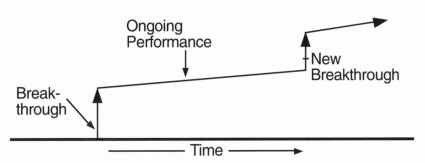

With Continuous Improvement

breakthrough gains. The following example shows how this works.

40 Percent Improvement
after a Breakthrough

Remember the Pentagon's infamous $600 toilet seat? It belonged to the Navy's P-3C anti-submarine patrol aircraft, which is the subject of this example. However, the story takes place after the scandal, and has an entirely different outcome.

The Jacksonville, Florida, Naval Aviation Depot faced a

critical problem in 1988. They had just won an open competition with a private aerospace firm to overhaul P-3Cs and refit them with new equipment. The losing firm told them, "You may have won, but you'll never be able to do the work at the price you quoted." At first, it seemed this might be true because the first few planes refitted came in way over budget. If this continued, the depot would lose the contract, and employees would lose their jobs.

Breakthrough. To solve the immediate crisis, a cross-functional team of supervisors and employees completely redesigned the sequencing of the 100+ tasks in the refitting process, and eliminated many major time-wasting steps. This saved 500 labor hours per aircraft, a breakthrough success in labor-intensive work such as this. By the fifth plane, costs were back in line with the original bid price.

Continuous improvement. Most organizations would have stopped right there, but not the depot. Depot executives also completely redesigned the job's management structure with TQM, which resulted in saving 1,200 additional labor hours. The new management system worked as follows:

- **Involving customers.** Before, on-site customer representatives simply did quality checks, reviewed cost reports, and authorized change orders. For this job, they were regularly asked ideas and made part of teams working on particularly difficult problems. Their input added new dimensions to creating improvements.

- **Teams and ownership.** Before the contract, crews of single-skill employees did only one part of an aircraft refit, and worked on every plane. Thus, no employee worked on any one plane from start to finish. For this job, employees were formed into small multi-skill teams responsible for all work done on a single aircraft. This created a sense of ownership and pride for the final product among the workers.

- **Rewards.** The ownership feeling was encouraged by having the teams engage in friendly and informal competitions to see who could develop the most improvements in productivity, efficiency, and quality. The rewards: T-shirts, jackets, caps, teaching the other teams, and, as one worker said, "that pat on the back you get."

- **Delegation of authority.** Before the breakthrough, foremen and supervisors handled all the administrative duties of shop floor operations. In the new system, team leaders, themselves employees, were given authority for tasks usually reserved for foremen: tool control, minor leave requests, and work assignments. According to one foreman, "This is the first project in my 24 years here that I've actually been able to manage instead of just doing paperwork and putting out fires."

Also, in the past, questions to customers frequently had to go through several layers of management before being answered. This meant delays and additional costs to work around a problem. In the new system, foremen and team leaders were encouraged to talk directly with on-site customer representatives, and foremen were allowed to make some customer-authorized changes without higher clearance.

- **Feedback.** Whereas before, only managers saw quality, schedule, cost, and material use reports, usually weeks after the fact, in the P-3C job performance data were quickly collected, analyzed, distributed, and discussed among managers, employees, and customers. The data were keyed to a computer graphic program of the work flows of the operation, which enabled speedy diagnoses of performance problems.

- **Ideas from employees.** Improvement ideas once came mostly from managers. Under the new system, team leaders asked each of their team members every week for suggestions on improvement. Since all workers were given a computer graphic printout of the work flow for their part of the process, they could point precisely to where improvements could be made. Thus, the team leaders came back with hundreds of practical ideas for speeding work, saving money, and improving quality.

Managers acted within days, and sometimes hours, to put these ideas into action. "We did this because we needed the improvements, not for morale purposes," said one manager. "But what more positive feedback can you give an employee than to immediately implement his or her suggestions?"

Results: By the ninth aircraft, Jacksonville surpassed its best-case projection for labor hours, and by the 30th plane had trimmed another 1,200 hours off the labor budget—40 percent less than originally planned. Today, production is well ahead of schedule, with record levels of quality and cost savings—all because of the hundreds of small "base hit" changes suggested by employees and customers.

Continuous Improvement as Part of BPR Strategy

Most BPR projects provide at least some opportunity to apply TQM methods of improvement. We will show where this is appropriate in a moment, but first let's compare the two approaches. Before making the comparison, though, we need to emphasize that BPR is a method, while TQM is a management philosophy. The purpose of BPR is to make a quantum leap in performance in a business process. TQM's purpose is to encourage and enable all people in an organization to make improvements, whether large or small, that will increase customer satisfaction. Thus, a TQM organization may use BPR when appropriate but does so in the context of the principles listed in Figure 8-1 above.

Similarities and Differences in BPR and TQM

Similarities. In many cases the methods and tools used for BPR and TQM are the same, such as the use of cross-functional teams. In BPR, these usually are *ad hoc* teams of managers and experts assembled for the life of a redesign project. In TQM, most often they are permanent teams of managers from all parts of a process, who meet regularly to plan and coordinate ongoing improvement. Sometimes, TQM uses short-term special project teams made up of managers, employees, suppliers, and often even customers, who focus on a part of a larger core business process.

Both BPR and TQM call for objective decision-making based on facts. Thus, teams working in both approaches may use measurement and analysis tools such as check sheets, cause-and-effect diagrams, bar charts, scattergrams, run charts, and control charts. During their meetings, members of both BPR and TQM teams use methods such as brainstorming and the nominal group technique to generate ideas and reach consensus on solutions.

Differences. The key differences between the two approaches are the scope and the underlying assumptions of each. In BPR, the focus of improvement is a large, cross-functional business process. In TQM, the focus normally is on smaller processes that make up a larger business process. However, mature TQM organizations always change their smaller processes with the larger ones in mind to ensure that all improvements maximize total performance.

In BPR, the assumption is that you almost always completely redesign the process. In TQM, *in general* you assume that the fundamental purpose and structure of a process will remain intact (sometimes, though, you challenge this assumption, and do redesign a process). In TQM, usually you focus on improving one or more parts of the process, such as its inputs (information and materials); transformation components (people, supplies, methods, machines, and environment); and outputs (again, information and material).

Using TQM Methods during BPR

Even when a business process is radically redesigned, some of its parts remain essentially the same as before. This was the case at AT&T since there was no way to design wave soldering out of the process. In such cases, TQM methods are useful for overcoming problems and speeding up operations.

Using TQM on non-BPR processes. Some organizations use TQM to improve processes that contribute to, but are not part of, processes that are the targets of BPR. Often, these include support processes found in accounting, administration, recruiting and hiring, and other such functions. TQM helps to improve operations in the parts of these other processes that affect the redesigned processes.

During "shakedowns." Quite often, a redesigned business process has to go through a "shakedown" phase once it starts operating. During this phase, you may need to solve many small problems in the new process. Teams of employees following the TQM approach often will be able to handle these "glitches."

Introducing TQM as Part of Redesigning a Process

Many organizations choose to use BPR as an opportunity to introduce TQM. In many ways, this is easier than introducing it to processes that are not being redesigned: everyone is more open to change in a new business process. In another way, it can be difficult since the nature of BPR often puts people in fear of their jobs and security, so that they are suspicious of any attempt to enlist them in ongoing improvement efforts. Here, we will go over the decisions you need to make before considering the integration of BPR and TQM, then discuss how to tie the two together.

Making a Commitment to TQM

No business process operates in isolation. Its performance is affected by other processes, by managers and employees who transfer into it from other parts of a company, and by the culture of the entire organization. Thus, in deciding to introduce TQM to one business process, you have to seriously consider doing the same for all or nearly all others.

Ideally, your organization will make the commitment to do this before the BPR project. However, you need not introduce TQM to all parts of your operations at once (few organizations do). Instead, you can use a BPR project as an opportunity to test and demonstrate the results of TQM, allowing everyone, from top management on down, to see the benefits of this approach.

The important thing is to follow through by introducing TQM to other processes. BPR can give you the momentum needed to do this: success breeds success.

The Elements of TQM

TQM has a number of necessary elements, which we describe and show how to integrate into a process during BPR.

Customer focus. All TQM organizations are by definition customer focused. This means that management continually evaluates how well an organization meets customer expectations, and reports this information to all managers and employees. In redesigning a business process, it is thus wise to build in policies, methods, and schedules for the routine assessment of customer expectations. This information needs to be communicated to all personnel, to let them know what customers want.

Within an organization, processes are said to have "internal" suppliers (the processes that provide them with work-in-progress) and "internal" customers (the processes that receive their work-in-progress). Most internal improvement is geared toward meeting the expectations of these internal customers and suppliers. This is one reason for the frequent use of cross-functional teams: they are an ideal way to bring together internal suppliers and customers to work on improvement issues.

Using cross-functional teams during BPR is an ideal way to introduce the internal customer/supplier concept. Also, training and allowing personnel to identify and communicate with their internal customers and suppliers solidifies this concept as basic to operational improvement.

Goals and objectives. Clear goals and objectives are needed for guiding TQM and might include:

- **Advancing past the breakpoint set during redesign.** For example, if the breakthrough goal was to decrease cycle time by a set amount, further decreases in time may be essential for maintaining the competitive advantage gained through redesign. Thus, a priority goal for TQM might be related to time and it might be phrased as: "Reduce through-put time every year."

- **Enhancing secondary factors in the process.** A redesign may be focused on achieving one or two breakpoints, but there are other factors important to the long-term success of a process. For example, the initial BPR goal may be to reduce cycle time, while factors such as saving money may have been given less consideration. Addressing these factors during the post-breakthrough period is appropriate and often necessary to maximize the impact of the redesign.

The value of such goals is that they give direction to the search for improvements. This helps people avoid pursuing, say, a potential energy-saving project, when energy costs are not a priority problem.

This type of goal-setting ideally should be designed into

ongoing process operations, done every year or every other year by the top management "owners" of a business process. Such a schedule thus should be part of the overall redesign plan, and should be set up to complement corporate-level strategic planning.

Management planning for improvement. With clear goals, middle managers can set objectives for improvement. In response to a goal of cycle time reduction, managers can analyze their smaller processes to determine which consumes the most time. Then they can focus their attention on this time-consuming process, and set measurable objectives and plans for reducing its cycle time. Like goal-setting, this calls for a regular planning schedule.

Training in improvement goals and objectives. If every employee is educated about the goals and objectives of the business process, then he or she is more likely to contribute to them. Such training can become part of the implementation phase of BPR. However, for maximum effect, this needs to be accompanied by the training discussed in the next paragraph.

Training in TQM methods. All TQM organizations train their managers and employees in improvement procedures. These include the use of the tools and methods mentioned earlier in this chapter, plus specialized tools appropriate for the type of work being done. Coopers & Lybrand believes that this training is most effective when it is applied immediately to actual improvement opportunities. Otherwise, many people will forget what they have learned.

Two points in the BPR process offer excellent opportunities for this type of training:

- Middle and later phases of BPR (i.e., *Redesign* and *Realize* phases in BreakPoint BPR). These phases provide many opportunities for management and employee teams to start using TQM tools. The Shreveport Works is a good example.

- During post-breakthrough shakedowns. As noted earlier, TQM tools and procedures can be used to stabilize a redesigned process once it is installed.

Formal training in job skills and tasks. Many organizations follow an unstructured on-the-job training system: someone who already performs a task teaches a new person how to do it. The result often is a passing-on of short cuts and mistakes from one generation of workers to the next. TQM organizations emphasize formal training for all new workers, so that all learn to work the same, correct way. Thus, it is a good idea to design in ongoing formal training during BPR and to budget the resources needed for this.

Teams. Teams are an integral part of TQM. Their primary benefits to an organization are better coordination, sharing of talent and creativity, and, for employees, the ability to manage operations with little supervision. BPR provides an ideal opportunity to determine the types of teams that are best for a process and for an organization.

These may range from the cross-functional management teams discussed earlier in this chapter, to employee teams that manage day-to-day operations in specific task areas. For example, Shreveport is now starting to use self-managed teams of employees, as have companies such as Federal Express, General Foods, and many others.

Feedback systems. In Chapter 9, we discuss the need for systems to measure process performance. Such systems are critical for TQM, and should provide employees with feedback on process factors such as cycle time, costs, defects, and customer satisfaction. However, most pre-BPR processes confine this information to management, which is like police having radar guns and cars not having speedometers.

Thus, while planning information systems during BPR, make sure they provide good feedback to the people who will operate the redesigned processes. One of the best ways to do this is to have employees collect and analyze data on their own operations. This may be as simple as having them review a sample of work-in-progress once a day or once a week.

Reward systems. Reward systems include individual performance appraisals, salary increases, promotions, bonuses, and other awards for ideas or outstanding performance. There are no hard-and-fast rules for developing reward systems under TQM, except that they need to be designed to promote such improvement. Thus, organizations that follow this approach tend to use the following practices:

- They collect hard data on process, team, and individual performance, which provide an objective basis for performance appraisal.

- They do away with annual performance reviews and switch to a continual review system where managers regularly counsel and coach employees.

- They reward team performance by dividing bonuses equally among team members.

- Individuals receive extra pay for learning new skills that contribute to their team's performance.

- Many use gainsharing plans, where part of the savings or increased revenues an organization gains due to TQM are shared among all employees.

- Most make frequent small rewards to individuals and teams, often no more than a token cash payment.

Most of all, these organizations are keenly aware of the types of manager and employee behavior they want to encourage. Thus, they use rewards to encourage risk taking, problem prevention, and discovery of new opportunities—all essential elements of TQM.

When is the best time to start introducing new reward systems? You can begin by offering team bonuses to the planning and design teams involved in your BPR effort. Then design effective reward systems into your new business processes— these will be as important as any technical feature of your new way of working.

BPR and TQM: The Long-Term Quick Fix

A recent *Wall Street Journal* cartoon showed one executive saying to the other, "What we need is a long-term quick fix." Although neither BPR nor TQM is as easy as we would like "quick fixes" to be, a strategy that combines the two comes about as close to a long-term quick fix as is humanly possible. BPR catapults you ahead of the competition, and TQM helps keep you there. It's a combination that's tough to beat.

Summary

- Organizations need continuous process improvement to maintain leadership in a turbulent world. Otherwise, process performance will decay; factors may change that render a process incapable of delivering good output; or competitors will catch up with and pass your current level of performance.

- TQM offers a way of maintaining positive dynamism in processes. It ensures the constant enhancement of performance, which will make it harder for competitors to surpass you.

- A TQM organization has a very different management style. Elements of this style include customer focus, direction from top management, teamwork at all levels, scientific decision-making, and new reward systems.

- BPR offers the opportunity to introduce TQM, both as a means of maintaining and enhancing gains in a process, and as a first step toward adopting TQM as a total corporate management style.

Breakpoint BPR: Beyond Process Improvement

SECTION HIGHLIGHTS

◆

An overview of
Coopers & Lybrand's BreakPoint BPR
methodology.

◆

Conducting BreakPoint BPR in your company.

◆

The characteristics of companies
that succeed.

141

The Breakpoint BPR Methodology

This section describes Coopers & Lybrand's proprietary methodology for planning and implementing BPR. BreakPoint BPR is a three-phase process that takes an interdisciplinary approach to creating breakthrough change. Our methodology is based on worldwide experience in helping companies define and attain new competitive advantage. In addition to reflecting the principles discussed in Section 2, key characteristics of BreakPoint BPR include:

Taking a Comprehensive Approach to Change

BreakPoint BPR is a unified methodology that uses operational, technical, and business knowledge to plan change. Core business process analysis provides a real link between the activities of an operation and its strategic objectives. Instead of relying on traditional structural methods of competitive positioning, such as market segmentation or product positioning, BreakPoint BPR revisits customer and shareholder expectations, cost dynamics, the role of information, and core competencies. Thus, a "results orientation" is built into plans for innovation.

Basing Change on Indisputable Facts

BPR design teams base their innovations on indisputable facts about the current situation: how processes work (or don't work); what the competition is doing; what customers and shareholders want; and organizational factors that may enable or disrupt innovation. Achieving consensus on facts such as these provides invaluable support for dramatic change.

Using Techniques that Foster Creativity

Taking a creative approach to product development, service delivery, or marketing is routine for most companies, but creating a whole new way of doing business is not. As BreakPoint BPR evolved, Coopers & Lybrand's management specialists recognized that the ability to generate revolutionary innovations was fundamental to success. While a methodology can't "create creativity," it can promote and evoke it. Breakpoint BPR includes several techniques to jump-start and support the creative process:

- Involving senior managers and senior consultants who are known for, and are experienced in, creative innovation.

- Using proven brainstorming techniques.

- Providing change models from competitors and other industries to seed creative adaptations.

- Using computer modeling and simulation through systems such as SPARKS to provide insights for innovative ideas.

Creating Sustainable Competitive Advantage and Lasting Organizational Change

As anyone who has ever tried to lose weight or stop smoking knows, it's a lot easier to make a change than it is to maintain it. Several features of Breakpoint BPR are designed to prevent organizational and competitive "relapse":

- Redesign options that will give a company a lead that competitors can't quickly overcome. Thus, redesign plans go beyond simply introducing new technology, which competitors also can buy. These redesign options include major changes in relationships among employees, managers, vendors, and even customers; organizational structures that differ from traditional hierarchies; a workforce with a new skill mix and approach to their jobs; and shifts in organizational culture and values. Because these are hard changes to make, they raise significant barriers to competitors who think they only need to buy new equipment to reach parity.

- Change management techniques described in Chapter 7 will guide and support managers and employees in adopting a new way of working and a new set of values.

- Companies can make the transition from BPR to continuous improvement. While incremental, steady improvement won't always create breakthroughs, it is essential to sustaining them.

CHAPTER 9

CREATING BREAKTHROUGHS

CHAPTER HIGHLIGHTS

◆

Discovering the breakpoints that will
produce competitive advantage.

◆

Determining which processes must be redesigned
to gain breakthroughs.

◆

Establishing a BPR project management structure.

◆

Assessing "as-is" process performance before BPR.

◆

Redesigning processes to produce breakthroughs.

◆

Managing change during BPR.

◆

Installing the redesigned process.

◆

Sustaining and increasing redesigned
process performance.

Discovering Where You Are,
How Much You Need To Change

Dun & Bradstreet, a major software and information services company, had established a strategic objective to help the company deal with difficult financial times: improving the cost effectiveness of its sales and sales support activities. To achieve that aim, a BPR project team developed plans to redesign four key business processes in the sales and support areas: contracts management, commission processing, "prospecting" for new customers, and territory management. They selected these processes for redesign because their multi-disciplinary assessment of the company's existing situation had suggested important opportunities for gaining new breakpoint advantage. For example:

- Of the average 2,742 minutes it took local Dun & Bradstreet offices to process one contract, only 220 minutes were spent actually working on the contract; the other 2,522 minutes consisted of "waiting time."

- The policy of renewing contracts and the timing of renewals contributed $4.8 million to the annual cost of contract management.

- Transfer processing added another $780,000 per year to contract management costs. Negotiation of transfers caused tension between national and district offices because policies on transfers were unclear.

- The approach to getting new customers was unstructured. As a result, existing customers received prospecting calls, different departments called the same prospective customers, and data had never been collected to assess the effectiveness of various prospecting techniques.

FIGURE 9-1

THE BREAKPOINT BPR PROCESS

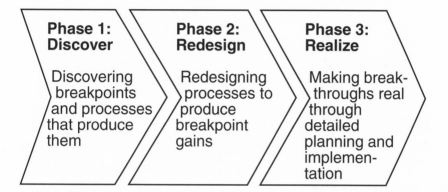

Phase 1: Discover	**Phase 2: Redesign**	**Phase 3: Realize**
Discovering breakpoints and processes that produce them	Redesigning processes to produce breakpoint gains	Making break-throughs real through detailed planning and implemen-tation

- Internal reporting at the territory manager level exceeded service industry norms and was inconsistent with the strategic goal of increasing Dun & Bradstreet's external customer focus.

The project team identified several potential breakpoints that process redesign could achieve; some were related to reduced cycle time and others to better organizational structure. In addition, projections showed that simplifying the contracts management process and moving to nonrenewable contracts would create a cost-breakthrough worth millions of dollars and eliminate duplicative information systems. Restructuring the way customer support needs were met could save even more. Overall, the cost savings goal was $13 million, a level of change that could positively affect Dun & Bradstreet's competitive position. Almost $10 million of these savings could be realized quickly and could help finance longer-term redesign efforts.

One further victory: contract processing went from ten days to one.

"Initial redesign activities gave Dun & Bradstreet a fact-based picture of its as-is situation," says Mike Blum, the Coopers & Lybrand partner who supervised support to this project. "This step is critical to establishing a solid foundation for change. Although some BPR rhetoric suggests that you 'obliterate' current processes or 'start with a clean sheet of paper,' the reality is that you have to start from where you are. Then you can assess how far you'll have to go to achieve a competitive advantage—and what you'll need to redesign to get there."

BreakPoint BPR

Figure 9-1 presents an overview of Coopers & Lybrand's proprietary methodology for planning and implementing business process redesign. As it shows, BreakPoint BPR is a three-phase process that takes an interdisciplinary approach to creating breakthrough change. Its steps are based on Coopers & Lybrand's worldwide experience in helping companies define and attain new competitive advantage.

While the BreakPoint BPR methodology is an organized approach to creating dramatic change, it is not a standard roadmap. The precise steps and chronology each company follows are tailored to its own unique goals, organization, and needs. In the rest of this chapter, we will show how its key features are usually applied.

Phase I — Discover: Where's the Breakthrough?

Activities and techniques used during the *Discover* phase of Coopers & Lybrand's BreakPoint BPR methodology are designed to answer that question, usually in two to four months' time. While the *Redesign* phase devises the innovations that create the breakthrough, *Discover* shows **where** breakthroughs are possible. Based on assessments of your company and its competitive environment, *Discover* also identifies the minimum level of change you'll need to put (and keep) your company out in front.

Starting from Strategy, not Scratch

Corporate strategy must be the starting point for breakthrough development because a strategic "to be" vision gives the company a consistent course. Strategic planning activities often reveal the need for dramatic change and may even immediately pinpoint the processes that need transformation. However the need for a BPR project is identified, its scope and direction need to support and link with the corporate vision of the future.

Most organizations have a strategic plan. To be a useful starting point for BPR, however, it needs to be based on:

- A thorough environmental and competitor analysis.

- A comprehensive understanding of the needs and capabilities of customers and suppliers.

- An objective analysis of the resources and capabilities of the organization.

- A well-founded projection of future sources of competitive advantage.

- Quantitative information that allows modeling of the revenue, cost, and resource implications of strategic alternatives.

- Widespread senior management consensus on the strategic vision.

The company's strategy should also include objectives in specific competitive dimensions, such as better meeting customer needs (attractive product features, service, price/positioning), superior economics (lower basic product/service costs, cost-to-serve advantage), or time (more timely delivery, faster new product development). Figure 9-2 lists additional competitive dimensions that frame BPR decisions. Major improvements in one or more of these may be the breakpoint that creates a competitive edge.

If key aspects of the strategic plan are missing, filling the gaps is an important first step. A clear understanding of what drives competitive advantage and where the company wants and needs to go are a critical element in BPR decisions. Chapter 4 discusses how to develop this understanding through:

- Customer research
- Competitive analysis
- Benchmarking
- Financial review
- Operational review
- Information management review
- Assessment of key performance indicators
- Organizational culture assessment (see also Chapter 7)

Identifying the BreakPoint

When Bendix Automotive Services Group of Allied-Signal Corporation wanted to expand its market for anti-lock brake systems, executives realized that if they could *cut the price* and *time-to-market* of anti-lock brake systems *in half,* they could capture and dominate the market in mid- and lower-priced cars.

A major semiconductor manufacturer *reduced its lead time for delivery* from more than a month to two days. This major service performance leap has enabled them to capture many competitors' customers over the last two years.

Fifteen years ago, a major credit card/financial services company gained a significant competitive edge when it moved into the *global market* with *cash machines* and *marketing* campaigns. Today, that breakpoint advantage has been exhausted, and they are assessing their services and operations to find a

FIGURE 9-2

KEY COMPETITIVE DIMENSIONS

Market Related	Product Related	Production Related	Finance Related
Reaching new customers	Time to develop	Cost of product	Cost of funds
Promoting product	New product	Quality of product	Source of funds
Time to market	Design of product	Lead time manufacture	Product financing
Responsiveness to change	Technology of product	Flexibility of production	Financial stability
Pricing of product	Support for the product	Process design	
Certification of product		Delivery reliability	
		Product differentiation	
		Product options	

new breakpoint that will help them leap ahead of the competition in the 1990s.

The Fibers Division of Allied-Signal Corporation *cut its cycle time from 16 weeks to two weeks* by developing a strategic alliance with a textile mill. By redesigning its processes to manufacture to order rather than to inventory, this also created the opportunity for *premium pricing at the point of sale.*

All of these companies successfully identified a market breakpoint that catapulted them ahead of the competition. As Figure 9-2 shows, many different types of breakpoints can produce high market impact or competitive financial advantage.

Defining an organization's own unique breakpoint involves answering two questions:

1. What do customers and shareholders value most highly? Making a major change that doesn't impress those you need to please won't produce breakpoint results. Thus, understanding customer preferences and priorities is essential to identifying the right breakpoint. BPR efforts may use customer surveys or live prototyping to get this type of information.

Sometimes proactive customer feedback about what they wish a company provided—or why they are changing to a competitor—provides the impetus to make a major change. For example, the Bank of Boston's securities transfer customers had expressed concern over what appeared to be a "loose," uncoordinated operation in multiple sites. They did not feel comfortable that their stock transfer documents were secure or that the process worked efficiently, based on cycle times that were longer than the industry standard and unpredictable. As described in Chapter 1, these concerns helped shape the consolidation of operations into one "flexible factory" setting that not only has improved efficiency, but also gives customers confidence in the quality of the service they receive.

FIGURE 9-3

BREAKPOINT OPPORTUNITY MAP

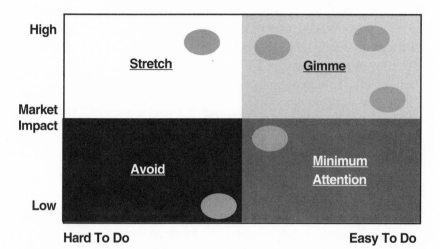

= Breakpoint Strategy

2. Can we achieve and sustain breakpoint performance? To answer this question, companies use process mapping and strategic performance assessments discussed in Chapter 4. These analyses help define the gap between current performance and breakpoint performance. They also allow evaluation of the competencies and resources that the company has to close the gap.

Identifying the breakpoint includes both a creative effort and a structured process of ranking potential breakpoints according to their desirability and achievability. Figures 9-3 and 9-4 illustrate two types of tools that companies create to rank breakpoint options.

"Decisions about breakpoints and which processes to change go hand-in-hand," says Coopers & Lybrand's Don King. "As you start to look at the levels of change you need to influence a market shift, you look at a lot of related 'what ifs.' What if we offered more product innovations? What if the product design process took two months instead of two years? What if we had the technology to automate some of the job? Questions like these move us away from a 'continuance' mentality and help us envision processes and results as they could be."

Choosing the Processes to Redesign

Identifying the breakpoint also involves making a preliminary decision on which processes to redesign. When Geon Vinyl determined that product specialization and reduced cycle time could improve its competitive position, for example, that focus implied a change in its production and materials management processes.

The reverse situation also occurs. When Dun & Bradstreet performed value-added analysis on its as-is processes, they discovered important opportunities for breakpoint-level change. Value-added analysis asks four key questions about the activities in a process:

1. Could this activity be eliminated if some prior activity were done differently (or correctly)?

2. Does the technology exist to eliminate this activity?

3. Could this activity be eliminated without harming the form, fit, or function of the customer's product?

A "yes" answer to any of these questions means that the activity does not add value.

4. Is this activity required by an external customer and will that customer pay for it?

FIGURE 9-4

KEY BREAKPOINT
DEPENDENCIES

Breakpoint Elements

Value Chain Enablers	Lead Time	Quality	Cost	Reliability	Process Design	Flexibility	Differentia- tion/Options
Facilities Network			X	X		X	
Sourcing	X					X	
Capacity Management	X		X				
Demand Driven Logistics	X		X	X			
Product "Technology"					X		X
Process "Technology"	X	X	X	X			X
Product Design	X	X	X		X		X
Quality	X	X			X		
Information Technology	X		X		X		
Cost Accounting			X		X	X	
Organization	X	X	X	X	X	X	X
Human Resources /Culture	X	X	X	X	X	X	X
Easy To Do	✓				✓		✓
Hard To Do		✓	✓	✓		✓	

Maximizing Creative Clout

To select breakpoints with the best potential:

● Hold creative strategy sessions that use proven brainstorming techniques.

● Don't limit breakpoint options based on current performance or technological constraints. Ideas developed in the *Redesign* phase may dramatically improve current operations or make radical changes that make current performance irrelevant.

● Spark creative thinking and inspire a sense of the possibilities by discussing the breakthroughs others have achieved. But don't stop there. Your creative thinking must go beyond the models to provide true advantage.

● Get radical. Don't be constrained by the seeming feasibility of a breakpoint. Dare to ask how customer value would be increased if you reduced cycle time from three weeks to one hour or if you cut costs by 90 percent. Setting these dramatic "stretch" targets will encourage creativity and innovation when the breakpoint team redesigns processes.

● Set tight deadlines. Defining the breakpoint should not be a time-consuming process because all the information you need should already have been gathered and analyzed.

● Keep the sustainability of competitive advantage in mind. The best breakpoint will be difficult for competitors to replicate or overcome any time soon.

This question is the ultimate measure of an activity's value; if the answer is "no," the activity is a good candidate for elimination. Eliminating processes that have no value to the customer, as Dun & Bradstreet did, can produce enormous competitive benefits, and may be the basis for redesigning an entire process.

Assessing "As–Is" Performance

Assessing the current performance and capabilities of existing business processes is an essential part of choosing which one(s) to redesign. Performance needs to be measured in terms of total cost, total cycle time, level of defects, or other factors important to achieving a breakpoint. If the gap between "as-is" performance and breakpoint performance is wide, then a particular process may be a prime candidate for redesign. However, a narrow gap may call for less radical change, especially if the process is capable of being sufficiently improved without altering its fundamental structure.

Setting Priorities

BreakPoint analysis should also include a prioritization of redesign needs. As Figure 9-5 illustrates, some processes will not produce breakpoint, but they may still be important to get— or keep—right. These non-breakpoint processes are ideal targets for other improvement methods, such as total quality management.

Setting Goals

Achieving breakpoint change requires radical performance improvement. Setting radically high objectives—which should be quantifiable—helps define the necessary scope of redesign. For example, the impetus for the insurance company's case manager concept, discussed in Chapter 3, was the ambitious goal of reducing staff-related costs by 40 percent without compromising service.

FIGURE 9-5

BREAKPOINT PRIORITIES

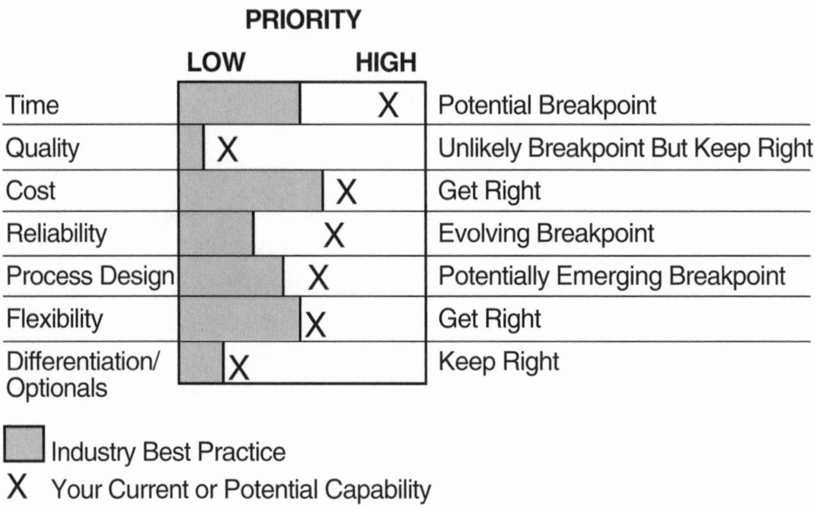

PRIORITY

	LOW	HIGH	
Time		X	Potential Breakpoint
Quality	X		Unlikely Breakpoint But Keep Right
Cost		X	Get Right
Reliability		X	Evolving Breakpoint
Process Design		X	Potentially Emerging Breakpoint
Flexibility		X	Get Right
Differentiation/ Optionals	X		Keep Right

☐ Industry Best Practice
X   Your Current or Potential Capability

"To attain this level of productivity improvement," says the former insurance company executive who was involved, "we knew we'd have to collapse whole processes into a single job, fuse separate systems into a single system. That goal made us think about how to empower each employee to do more."

The box at right summarizes the types of BPR objectives set by different industry sectors, reported in a recent Conference Board survey.

Selected BPR Objectives
by Industry Sector*

Service
- Reduce 4-day turnaround for pricing to same day.
- Eliminate customer call-back by 20 percent.
- Reduce printed report distribution operation by 60 percent.
- Single point of contact for customers.

Manufacturing
- 100 percent on-time delivery.
- 85 percent reduction in order entry cycle time.
- 89 percent reduction in order entry auditing.
- 67 percent reduction in administrative shipping errors.
- Reduce time spent by 50 percent in "quote-to-ship" cycle support functions.

Banking and Insurance
- Reduce staff from 60 to one.
- Reduce check production costs by 50 percent.
- Target $100 million cost reduction from $650 million baseline.
- 100 percent system availability.

*Source: The Conference Board

Mapping "As-Is" Business Processes

A business process is a series of activities or steps that create products or services for customers.

Because a company's business processes are the key to its competitiveness, it is critical to have a consensus on how processes operate now. Coopers & Lybrand's "quick mapping" approach creates a high-level map that shows the major steps in the major processes and the path they take from start to finish.

159

These early models provide a baseline for more detailed mapping that may occur in the *Redesign* phase, and for envisioning dramatic changes that can lead to breakthroughs. For example, Figure 9-7 shows the types of changes that can occur when redesigning the process shown in Figure 9-6.

"The question everyone asks," says Coopers & Lybrand partner Helen Ojha, "is how detailed should the process map be? One answer is: How much detail can you justify *not* having? On the one hand, you have top executives with a 'Swiss Alps syndrome,' where they perch up in their suites, look down on the company, and say, 'Looks easy to change from here!' On the other hand, you have middle managers who become bogged down in process detail and say, 'It's impossible to change!' The key is to balance the two points of view. Executives cannot afford to stay up on their mountains, and managers have to get out of the weeds.

"Our SPARKS process modeling software helps us strike that balance. By automating many of the labor-intensive tasks in process mapping, it gives adequate process detail quickly and efficiently. You can use the simulation to identify opportunities for improvement *and* to project the impact of possible alternatives to help you decide what to change."

Change Management

As discussed in Chapter 7, successful BPR means changing more than processes or the business situation; it depends on effectively managing the human and cultural aspects of changes. Each phase of BreakPoint BPR includes major attention to change management issues. During the *Discover* phase, the three major issues are:

- **Design team composition.** These are the people who will plan the redesign. Besides having the requisite technical skills and process knowledge, many team members should come from within the business process

FIGURE 9-6

"AS IS" QUICK MAP OF
ORDER-TO-CASH PROCESS

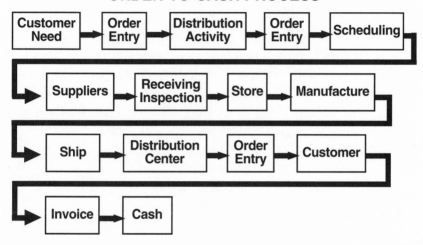

FIGURE 9-7

"TO BE" QUICK MAP OF
ORDER-TO-CASH PROCESS AFTER BPR

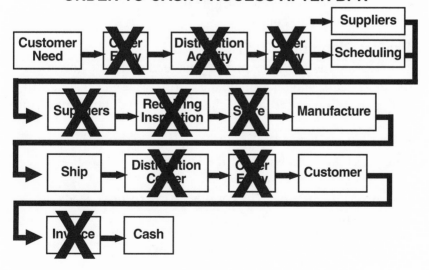

161

being redesigned. If, as noted in Chapter 5, they are the "best and brightest" people in a process, chances are they influence the opinions of peers and subordinates. This influence helps promote acceptance of change by non-team personnel.

- **Communication.** As indicated in Chapter 7, the type of research and planning conducted during the *Discover* phase will not have gone unnoticed by the workforce. At the end of the *Discover* phase (or even better, *during* it), executives must plan for effective communication with managers and employees about the nature of the changes to come and the reasons for them. Starting the *Redesign* phase without good communication will inevitably cause resistance to efforts by the redesign team to gather needed information.

- **Planning for displacement.** As also noted in Chapter 7, process redesign can lead to major displacement of the existing workforce. The *Discover* phase should be the starting point for developing policies and procedures for handling this development. These policies facilitate communication with personnel about the changes to come.

Project Planning: The Right Stuff

During the *Discover* phase, you need to decide how to organize, staff, and coordinate the effort. These decisions will vary depending on the size of the company and the scope of the redesign.

As discussed in Chapter 4, important points to consider when deciding who will staff the Discover phase are:

- Make sure the CEO or other top executive leads the effort;

- Build a team of top executives and managers from key

areas of the organization; and

- Include your "best and brightest" people in this phase and throughout the BPR project.

Aside from stressing the importance of the project, staffing it in this manner ensures the participation of key decision-makers and people with influence. This helps to guarantee their acceptance and support of the major changes that follow, changes that can affect their power and career advancements.

Figure 9-8 is an example of a BPR project management structure, adapted from a Coopers & Lybrand client who is redesigning several business processes.

The Steering Committee helps to carry out the first steps of the *Discover* phase, and later reviews recommendations from the redesign teams, offers them guidance, and acts to implement the needed changes. It is important to note that many Steering Committee members also serve on the Core Redesign Team and some lead the individual business process teams. This is an excellent example of change leadership, as discussed in Chapter Seven.

Top executives need to set up a schedule and budget for the *Discover* phase. However, while the budget may be flexible, the schedule should be adhered to as closely as possible. This is because the most precious resource in creating a breakthrough is time. Stretch out the *Discover* phase, and competitors will beat you to the punch.

Discover Phase Results Checklist

Before going on to the *Redesign* phase, it is best to have established or identified the following items during the *Discover* phase:

- A project management structure for the BPR process.
- A strategic assessment of the various factors that influ-

enced the choice of a breakpoint and that help determine organizational readiness for change.

- One or more breakpoint targets.

- One or more business processes that, if redesigned, will help achieve a breakpoint.

- An assessment of the "as-is" performance of the selected business processes

- A high- to medium-level model of the "as-is" and "to-be" business processes.

- A procedure for identifying process redesign team members.

- A communication plan for informing managers and employees about the changes to come and the reasons for them.

- At least a start on policies and procedures for employee displacement.

Items not discussed in this chapter, but that are still necessary, include:

- A schedule and budget for each redesign project, and for any corporate-wide coordination of multiple projects.

- If information technology *(IT)* is to play a role in the redesign, in-house and outside *IT* experts need to be involved in all phases of the *Discover* phase. They should develop an assessment of the role of *IT* in the redesign effort, identifying *IT* and the costs and timing of systems engineering or re-engineering planning. If high-level process analysis provides sufficient detail, an appropriate information model should be developed to

FIGURE 9-8

ORGANIZATION AND STAFFING
OF MULTI-PROJECT BPR EFFORT

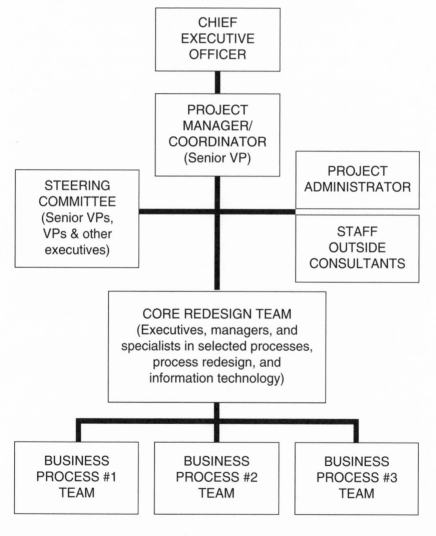

Each team is led by an executive, and includes
managers, key employees, and technical specialists.

guide further process redesign and systems engineering.

- A plan for communicating about the upcoming changes with customers, vendors, shareholders, and others.

- If outside consultants are to be used during subsequent phases, their services should be retained during the *Discover* phase.

- It may be that you have not yet introduced continuous improvement practices into your organization (see Chapter 8). If you intend to do so as part of BPR, now is the time to begin making a commitment to corporate-wide acceptance of this management approach. Redesigned processes are excellent pilot projects for continuous improvement. However, you cannot maintain these practices in one or a few business processes if the other processes do not follow suit.

Phase II — Redesign: Planning the Breakthrough

The *Redesign* phase of BreakPoint BPR involves all the skills and management abilities inherent in the design of any physical product or service. This is because its purpose is to plan every facet of a redesigned process, including its core and support structures, management system, human resources, work flow, and information technology. Also, a redesign effort may include identifying new values and organizational culture that are aligned with new methods of working.

Project Management for Redesigning a Single Process

Redesign teams. The people selected to redesign a business process must represent the skills and backgrounds needed for their project. Also, most business processes operate across organizational boundaries and involve many departments and work units. Therefore, members of the redesign team should be cross-functional: they should already work in the most important parts of the process.

Every team needs a leader. Wise organizations choose the "owner" of the "to-be" business process: the executive or top manager who will be in charge of the process after redesign. This ensures the "owner's" total commitment to superior results.

Often, teams are augmented by outside consultants who play several roles. As discussed in Chapter 5, these roles can include coach, facilitator, or technical specialist.

Parallel development. In modern design and redesign management, many development tasks are managed in parallel, as in concurrent or simultaneous engineering. This means that team members can address at once many different parts of a redesign, such as information technology, work flows, and human resources.

This approach, followed by BreakPoint BPR, reduces redesign lead time and costs. If done well, parallel development also ensures against hand-off errors and miscommunication inherent in strictly sequential development. Furthermore, it encourages synergy among team members, which produces transformational results such as those discussed in Chapter 6. Your keys to success in this parallel approach: excellent communication among all members of the team, and a master plan for development that integrates changes as redesign progresses, not when it ends.

Team building and team training. The diversity of team members and the need for parallel development requires superior teamwork; achieving this is the first task of a team that uses BreakPoint BPR. Usually led by an experienced facilitator/instructor, members "build" their team by clarifying goals and expectations and agreeing on a set of rules for team conduct. Through team-building exercises, they develop a team dynamic conducive to cooperation and synergy. The ultimate outcome is agreement on the procedures the team will follow in its work, which should include reporting and control, tools and techniques, and roles and responsibilities.

Since the team often uses tools and techniques that are new to its members, an instructor/facilitator leads them through the initial application of these methods to real-life issues that are part of the redesign effort. This "just-in-time" training ensures better learning than by rote instruction. Often, the facilitator will remain with the team over several weeks or months, coaching the members in tools and methods and facilitating meetings.

Why do all this? Because the redesign team is your single most valuable resource in BPR. A poorly coordinated team will result in major delays and problems, so investing in good teamwork is money well spent.

Setting Design Parameters

If these were not set during the *Discover* phase, you may want to establish some basic design parameters before starting redesign. These will govern your decisions about redesign alternatives. Some examples of parameters include:

- Centralize (or decentralize) operations whenever possible.

- Follow a certain process model [i.e., the flexible factory or just-in-time (JIT) cycle time reduction].

- Shift responsibility for some types of tasks to customers or suppliers.

- Provide easy information access to employees, managers, customers, suppliers, and other members of the enterprise.

- Minimize supervision.

- Outsource non-critical activities when cost effective.

- Tie performance measures to customer or shareholder satisfaction.

- Use information technology to guide employee decision-making.

- Design flexibility into all processes.

- Provide a single point of contact for customers or suppliers.

- Build continuous improvement into all processes.

Some of the above rules may not apply to your situation. The challenge is to develop parameters that are best for your processes and organization.

"As-Is" Process Mapping

This is a key information-gathering stage of *Redesign*. In the *Discover* phase, process mapping was done at a high- to medium-level, to select processes for redesign and establish objectives for them. In *Redesign,* teams do more detailed mapping of "as-is" process structure, which helps break a process down into more manageable units. Mapping also provides details of the different activities within a process, inputs and outputs, resources used, costs, and value-added and non-value-added tasks.

You may not need all the detail this section discusses, especially if you are about to completely transform a business process into an operation totally different from its "as-is" structure. However, even if many activities will be eliminated during redesign, it may be wise to map down to a level of detail that identifies activities such as those shown in the right-hand column of Figure 9-9 for the following reasons:

- Without this information, you may inadvertently "lose" a key activity that should be part of the "to-be" process design.

- It is important to know which work units and people will be affected by the redesign.

- Other processes may provide inputs to the one being mapped, such as information or materials. Parts of these processes may have to be redesigned or enhanced to meet the higher performance or different needs of the "to-be" process.

- Knowing the current resources devoted to each activity and, by extension, each business process, helps in doing cost/benefit analysis of alternative redesign options.

Activity analysis. Since manufacturing processes have long been subject to industrial engineering, it is often easy to obtain activity-level information on them. This is less true for service and white-collar processes: they tend to "grow, spread, and mutate" without documenting their work flows. In these latter cases, you may need to use an approach such as activity-based costing (ABC) or activity analysis to identify all relevant operations and the resources devoted to them.

By-the-book activity-based costing may be too time-consuming in a redesign effort. In BreakPoint BPR, Coopers & Lybrand sometimes uses an abbreviated ABC approach that locates all activities and generates approximate resource levels devoted to them. In the data-gathering phase, you first identify the departments and work units involved in a business process. Through interviews with managers, you locate the activities that make up the process. Then you ask people who work on the activities to estimate the percentage of a normal work year that they spend on these tasks (you can verify this, but usually it is on-target). Since service and white-collar operations are labor-intensive, multiplying these time percentages by annual salaries is a decent approximation of cost.

This investigation can produce some surprises. For example, a shipyard asked Coopers & Lybrand to conduct an ABC

FIGURE 9-9

ACTIVITY BREAKDOWN OF
"MATERIAL SUPPORT"
BUSINESS PROCESS

Business Process Purpose:
Acquires and Distributes Materials Used in Ship Overhauls

PROCESSES	SUB-PROCESSES	ACTIVITIES
Identify material Order/expedite material	Conduct inspections Conduct materials analysis	Receive material Identify material Store material (temporary)
Receive/inspect/ evaluate/ certify material	Process transaction (receiving and shipping)	Inventory warehouse Segregate by delivery point
Reject/cancel/ resolve/dispose material	Receive/store material	Load material for delivery
Maintain material information	Provide material support (materials for repairs, calibration, salvage, etc.)	Clean up receiving area
Other material support	Provide material support ("O" rings)	
	Provide material support (check material accuracy)	

analysis of several business processes done by its support departments. One process included job order planning for ship overhauls. Everyone assumed that most job order activities would be found in the planning departments. But, in fact, one half the people who participated in this process were *outside* these departments. This discovery had major implications for projects aimed at improving job order planning.

"As-Is" Process Performance and Capability

During the *Discover* phase, you took a high-level look at process performance and capability, and determined that they were inadequate for reaching the desired breakpoint. If you plan to retain parts of the process in the "to-be" redesign, you will want to take a more detailed look at their performance. Although they may remain basically intact, these parts can probably benefit from process improvement. An example of this was the wave-soldering operation at the Shreveport Works discussed in Chapter 8. Also, you may want to look at the performance and capability of the parts of other processes that provide inputs to the one being redesigned.

Generating Redesign Ideas

Once you know the status quo, you can decide how to change it. Although some decisions may have been made during the *Discover* phase, *Redesign* is when you add the details. Benchmarking, technical advice, trade literature, and other outside sources of information can help at this stage. After digesting this information, you need to add your own creative ingenuity to the design options available. At this point, challenging fundamental assumptions about the "as-is" process, "blue skying," team brainstorming, and asking "what if . . ." takes outside concepts to much higher levels of potential performance. Only when all ideas are out on the table should you begin to analyze their feasibility and value. Swatting down any ideas as they arise is a sure way to kill team creativity.

You also can use an "as-is" model of an existing process to determine how best to streamline and rationalize it. Here, a computerized simulation program such as Coopers & Lybrand's SPARKS can be quite useful. SPARKS creates a model of process elements, work flows, and resources, which is used to dynamically simulate the results of alternative changes to operations.

Having outside experts take part in the idea generation process is a good idea, since they can add fresh insights. Also, this is the time to make doubly sure your process redesigners and information technology *(IT)* people are synergizing. Otherwise, you will not achieve the full transformational effect of simultaneous consideration of business requirements and *IT* capabilities discussed in Chapter 6.

Quick Fixes

During the *Redesign* phase, you will probably discover many minor (and a few major) problems and opportunities that can be addressed before starting up a redesigned process. If solving these does not interfere with the new design, don't hesitate to get people to work on them immediately.

Testing Redesign Alternatives

Mapping and modeling. Mapping and modeling a proposed process redesign are good first steps in testing its feasibility (once again, this can be facilitated through computer simulation). There are two objectives to this: to thoroughly understand the redesign, and to test it against different assumptions. Also, mapping and modeling helps identify bottlenecks and potential flaws that need to be eliminated, and the types of inputs the process will require.

Financial and technical analysis. The second phase of testing involves cost estimating, cost/benefit analysis, and technical analysis. This information weeds out all but one or two alternatives, but there are still a few questions to ask.

Other analyses. The remaining questions are:

- Is your organization capable of using the proposed process? If not, what must be done to make it capable?

- What are the reactions of employees, managers, customers, suppliers, or other people affected by the process?

- What are the potential negative side-effects of using the proposed process? Can they be overcome?

If a redesign alternative survives these questions, then it is ready for detailed planning, taking into account the human and other resources needed to operate the new process.

Pilot testing. As discussed in Chapter 4, consider pilot testing a redesigned process. Often, you can operate a scaled-down version of a redesign alternative in one area of your organization, even without the support of new information technology. Besides helping spot the "bugs" in the redesign, people who use it are certain to offer improvement suggestions. This includes customers, who will be the ultimate judges of the value of the new way of working. Also, pilot tests serve to demonstrate the benefits of a new process to your workforce, which can help overcome resistance to change.

Developing the Information Model

A systems engineering tool, an information model is an overlay of the redesigned process showing its nerves and sometimes parts of its arms, legs, and brain. The model indicates the types of information flows needed to support the process, and often includes components that automate previously manual tasks. The model will guide subsequent work in planning information systems engineering, acquisitions, installation, and maintenance.

Usually, creating the information model follows the development of the detailed process model. However, the more parallel the planning of both models, the greater the likelihood of maximizing their synergy. This requires excellent teamwork between systems engineers and process redesigners.

Redesign Phase Checklist

At the end of this phase, you should have:

- Models and plans for the redesigned process and its supporting information systems.

- Cost/benefit and other assessment information on the "to-be" process and information system.

- An understanding of the types of changes that may be needed in other processes that provide inputs or receive outputs from the redesigned process.

In addition, you will probably have a wealth of information on other potential redesign ideas. Over time, use them to increase performance in the new process or others that provide inputs or receive outputs from it.

Items not discussed in this chapter, but that are still necessary, include:

- Receiving top-level approval for the redesign, and obtaining resources to support its introduction.

- A communication plan for informing employees, customers, suppliers, and other enterprise members about the redesign and its benefits to them.

- An assessment of change management requirements, and a plan for addressing them. (see Chapter 7).

Phase III — Realize: Making the Breakthrough

If a good job has been done in the *Discover* and *Redesign*

175

phases, you will find that the technical aspects of *Realize,* the implementation phase, are much easier. However, since the new process often fundamentally alters the way people work, you must give particular attention to change management.

New Teams

It is a good idea at this point to organize implementation teams made up of people who will be working in the "to-be" process. You will be able to identify them now, so including them in the transition period is logical. The more people you can involve in this phase, the better, since this encourages acceptance of change. At least some of the redesign team members should stay with these new teams, often as their leaders. These new teams will benefit from the team building and training in the *Redesign* phase.

Detailed Planning

You will need to flesh out the "to-be" process and information models, with input from the new team members. This includes determining resource requirements, technical fine-tuning, communications with other processes, and all the other details of putting the final touches on a new operation.

Having done this, it is wise to confirm the cost/benefit analysis done during the Redesign phase. In addition, you will want to set up performance measures for the new process, at a level of detail sufficient for its control and improvement.

Implementation Planning

This involves creating a detailed plan for transition from the "as-is" to the "to-be" process. Our experience is that most organizations' existing project planning systems are adequate for this task (with the exception of change management, discussed below). However, some consideration must be given to the cross-functional nature of the redesigned business process. It will operate across departmental boundaries, so introducing it needs superior coordination. The logical focal point for this is the new process "owner," who will be supported by implementation team members.

Change Management

Chapter 7 discussed in detail the types of change management planning and procedures needed to ensure the successful introduction of a redesigned process. One of these is a detailed assessment of the effects the redesign will have on the organization and its people. Following this assessment, you will need to create a change management plan. This should include new skill mix requirements, management systems, training needs, potential displacement issues, and other related factors.

A major part of change management during this phase is communicating the vision of the new process to your employees. This is best done face-to-face with managers first, followed by lower-level employees, in sessions that explain the rationale for the change, its benefits to them, and steps being taken to assist those who will be adversely affected by the change.

Installing the New Process

Technically, this will be executing implementation tasks according to plan. However, any complex change is bound to have a few "glitches," both during installation and immediately after. Also, other processes that are connected with the new one may require more minor modifications or enhancements to adjust to its new level of performance. As discussed in Chapter 8, these can be opportunities to further involve people in perfecting the new way of working. If you intend to introduce continuous improvement (or already practice it), these small problems are ideal for manager or employee teams to resolve.

Also, take care to make sure that people start out on the right foot, by using the process as intended. Formal training with close attention by management for several months afterward is the best way to ensure they know how to use the process properly.

Following installation, start measuring increased performance. As quickly as possible, you will want to confirm the cost/benefit calculations done earlier. And get ready for a pleasant surprise: your attention to all the details—technical, organizational, and human—almost certainly will deliver even better results than you anticipated.

Sustaining the Change

An unmonitored process soon decays in its performance, or develops the earlier mentioned tendency to "grow, spread, and mutate." Without good performance measures and management attention, your breakthrough gains will slowly unravel until you are once again behind the competitive eight-ball.

There are two ways to address this: strictly maintain the status quo of the new process or encourage continuous improvement. Doing the former is like coasting, and the only way to coast is downhill. You will be far better served to continue the uphill climb of continuous improvement (albeit on a milder slope) to long-lasting competitive advantage.

Realize Results Checklist

After the *Realize* phase, you should have:

- A breakthrough process that is fully documented, continually measured on its performance, and constantly improving.

- People who, as team members and individuals, have helped make one major change, and thus are trained and able to make other changes.

- A new set of values and an organizational culture that will help build the breakthrough organization described in Chapter 10.

Summary

- BreakPoint BPR is a three-phased approach to developing process breakthroughs. The phases are:

  ○ *Discover.* Identify breakpoints or target levels of performance that will provide long-lasting competitive advantage, then determine the process(es) that will help achieve the breakpoints.

  ○ *Redesign.* Assess the performance and structure of the "as-is" process, then redesign it and information systems to gain breakthroughs.

  ○ *Realize.* Plan the new process in detail, along with its installation, how to marshall support and acceptance for the new way of working, and how to sustain and increase breakthrough gains.

- This is a team-based approach to change, eventually involving everyone from executives to employees. Teams ensure that the needs of different parts of a cross-functional process are considered and met, as well as increase the acceptance of change.

- BreakPoint BPR encourages the parallel development of technical, information, and human systems during process redesign. This helps avoid downstream problems and promotes transformational thinking about breakthroughs.

- Changes made during BreakPoint BPR to the organization's values and culture help establish an organization capable of making dramatic improvements on demand.

CHAPTER 10

WHAT IT TAKES TO BE A BREAKTHROUGH ORGANIZATION

CHAPTER HIGHLIGHTS

True breakthroughs require vision, creativity, attitude, and the right type of organization. Of these requisites, the right organization is the most valuable.

◆

The breakthrough organization has the following characteristics:

- The desire to dominate, not match, the competition.
- An external viewpoint gives direction to improvement.
- Suffers no delays in its pursuit of excellence.
- Sees BPR as a growth strategy.
- Has a culture that values customers, shareholders, suppliers, and employees.
- Recognizes change as a business need.
- Understands its own capacity for change.

The most valuable core competency is the ability to create change.

Lessons from Edison

In the introduction to this book, we pointed out that Thomas Edison created an organization capable of routinely making breakthroughs, and therein lies the real secret of his success. This was the first modern R&D laboratory, which Edison called his "invention factory." Edison had a clear vision of what he wanted this laboratory to be: an organization of people and processes that could turn out at least one innovation every day, and a blockbuster invention every week.

We have certainly benefited from Edison's inventions. But we owe him a greater debt for showing us that what really counts is to have an organization capable of producing breakthroughs on demand. Let's see what that means in today's turbulent economic environment.

Characteristics of Breakthrough Organizations

A breakthrough organization has seven characteristics that differentiate it from the "wannabes" in the quest for high performance. These characteristics do not include deep pockets or hordes of experts as eager to tear down as they are to build up. Instead, these seven qualities can be developed in any organization, regardless of size or resources.

1. Obsessed with winning

Few disagree that Wayne Gretzky is the world's greatest-ever hockey player. Asked why he dominates the ice, Gretzky says, "The other players skate to the puck. I skate to where the puck is going to be." It's the same with a breakthrough organization: the objective is always to be in the right place before your competitors. Drawing even with the competition is not the objective—to Gretzky, that's skating with the pack, not dominating it.

BreakPoint BPR is about dominance: being obsessed with

winning and beating, not meeting the competition. Today, doing otherwise means someone else is going to dominate you. In a breakthrough organization, everyone understands and is ready to act on this hard, cold fact.

Achieving this obsession with winning throughout an organization is not easy. Most people's attitude is, "We want improvement, but not that much improvement." Thus, they say they'll "do their best, but . . . ." Winston Churchill knew how devastating that attitude could be, when in World War II he told embattled Britons: "It is not enough to do your best; you must do what must be done."

President Bill Adler gave the same message to his top managers when preparing PHH FleetAmerica for BPR. "Unfortunately, those who could not accept radical change are no longer here," he told Coopers & Lybrand. "We created a new leadership team that believes in change and will make it happen."

An obsession to win was also achieved among employees at AT&T facilities all across the country, including the Shreveport Works discussed in Chapter 8. For example, the employees are so driven to win that they hold parades (an employee's idea, not management's) with floats and banners that declare their intention to "Beat the Competition!" not "Try a little harder." This attitude, more than anything else, is why two years ago *Fortune* magazine recognized an AT&T factory as one of five prime examples of world-class manufacturing in the United States.

2. "Not invented here" is a plus, not a penalty

After a while (especially if they are good at what they do) some organizations develop a "not invented here" attitude. They turn inward for new ideas, and trust their instincts to "know" what customers want, so they feel there is no need to ask. This attitude is the road to ruin and has no place in a breakthrough organization.

As discussed in Chapter 4, breakthrough organizations seek inspiration and ideas outside their walls as well as within. This is the reason for BreakPoint BPR's heavy, up-front focus on determining customer expectations, asking trend-setting customers about new ideas, scrutinizing what the competition is doing, and benchmarking best practices wherever they may be.

In addition, BPR is a learning process, and companies that practice it are learning organizations. Their people routinely participate in professional or trade associations and outside conferences and courses, both as students and teachers. They consider it as important (or more important) to read trade journals as the company newsletter or the latest internal memo. Such organizations invest heavily in all forms of training and professional education because they know their greatest competitive advantage comes from the minds of their personnel.

3. Suffers no delays in the pursuit of excellence

Breakthrough organizations are always ready and able to mobilize for major change because they know that, today more than ever, radical improvement of critical business processes cannot wait. Thus, their leaders demand that BPR projects proceed at top speed, and they provide the people and resources to make this happen. Remember, if you take years to create a breakthrough, it's no longer a breakthrough.

4. Sees BPR as a growth strategy

The breakthrough organization sees BPR as a growth strategy, not simply as a means to cut costs or downsize. It understands that cost-cutting by itself may increase profits in the short term, but without improving operations it will probably lose customers, not win new ones.

Thus, such organizations use BPR first on the core business processes that enable them to serve customers better and faster, secure in the knowledge that doing so almost always reduces costs as well. They apply it to other, less important areas, too, but always with the objective of increasing performance in core business processes.

5. Values customers, shareholders, employees, suppliers, and other members of its enterprise

To the breakthrough organization, there is no conflict between the desires of any of these constituencies. They are united in a quest for high performance and customer satisfaction because this means success for all. The following values alert the breakthrough organization to the need for change, and give direction and support to that change.

The breakthrough organization:

Values its customers by constantly seeking ways to create value for them. Today, quality is the baseline; you have to go beyond it to truly create extra value for customers. This means heavy investment in research and testing of new ideas that delight customers, not just satisfy them. It means a constant search for new ways to add value not only to products and services, but also to your relationship with customers. The key is using objective research (not gut feelings) to anticipate what customers will want tomorrow as well as today—if you don't, someone else will. Finally, valuing customers means everyone in the organization accepts that customers are the final arbiters of your future.

Values its shareholders by investing in business processes that will yield high return on investment, profits, and competitive advantage. This is not a simple proposition, especially in an organization that permits its divisions and departments to independently decide, without benefit of top-level corporate strategy, where to invest improvement resources. Shareholders want to see these investments strategically directed toward improvements that maximize stock value growth and dividends, not for minimal savings in some minor operation. At a minimum, valuing shareholders focuses BPR investments on reducing non-value-added work, the savings from which go into dividends and more investment in creating competitive advantage. Substitute better public service for ROI and tax savings for profits, and you have the shareholder (read John Q. Public) values of the breakthrough government agency.

Values its employees because, in the end, they are the ultimate competitive advantage. Other companies can buy the same technology as you, and can imitate your processes. What they can't buy is an organizational culture that supports competition, integrity, trust, inventiveness, teamwork, openness, and an obsession with winning. Without these qualities, employees cannot be expected to take the risks needed for breakthrough improvement. Instead, they will become narrow, risk-averse, bean-counting clock punchers. But if they trust their organization to do the right thing, and if it trusts them, together they become a breakthrough team that thrives on change.

Values its suppliers by including them in the process of change, instead of forcing them to accept it after the fact. The breakthrough organization understands that, for its most critical business processes, a few preferred suppliers willing to go the extra mile are worth more than a raft of "it's-not-in-the-contract" low-bidders. In this relationship, both buyer and seller are equally committed to breakthroughs, even if it means major changes for the supplier. The buyer invests in the supplier through long-term contracts that in turn motivate the supplier to invest in new capabilities. Often, breakthrough organizations give technical assistance and even direct financial aid to their suppliers.

In much the same way as suppliers, the breakthrough organization values the other members of its enterprise, such as distributors and trading partners. This is because such organizations understand that breakthroughs often require enterprise-wide change—team action by everyone involved in a product or service life cycle.

6. Structures itself for change

The breakthrough organization is equipped to survive and prosper in the turbulent 1990s because it is built around the only constants in this decade: change, change, and more change. Employees are selected for their ability to learn, and are trained for flexibility so they can adjust to new ways of working. Technology and information systems are built for ease of maintenance and upgrade, so that their capabilities can be improved when needed. Even the very structure of this type of organization is designed for change: horizontal, flexible, modular, and ready at any time to accommodate new products and new processes.

Finally, the executives of the breakthrough organization practice change leadership (see Chapter 7). They personally participate in planning and implementing changes, find the resources for them, and take pains to reward those who make change happen. How can you best judge such leaders? Look at their calendars: they spend most of their time raising performance for competitive advantage—not managing the status quo.

7. Is aware of its change potential

This final characteristic is found only among the very best organizations: they know their capability to produce breakthroughs. Armed with this knowledge, they can at once explore and exploit many opportunities for competitive advantage, while rivals struggle with a mere few.

This applies to all business processes, so that breakthrough potential can be continually developed. Also, understanding this capacity for change encourages the use of pilot tests of alternative approaches to breakthroughs, which lets customers evaluate tangible results and suggest further improvements. Thus, such organizations can make the commitment to a breakthrough (which always bears some risk) based on customer confirmation of its value.

Understanding change potential also applies to the organization as a whole. Seeking this knowledge, the mature organization studies its culture; its capability to recruit, train, and retain the right employees for the future; and its ongoing relationship with customers, stockholders, and suppliers. Finally, such organizations routinely and rigorously review their approach to BPR, and constantly strive to improve it.

Using BPR To Create the Breakthrough Organization

If your organization already has these seven characteristics, you are in fine shape for the future. However, remember that these qualities require continual nurturing and support. Otherwise, they will have disappeared when you need them most.

But if you are not quite there yet, your next BPR project is the best opportunity to instill these qualities in your organization (hopefully, our book has shown you how). Done right, BPR creates a window of opportunity for accomplishing more than just one breakthrough. Use it to begin redesigning not only how you plan for change, but also your relationship with customers and suppliers, and even the culture and values of your entire organization. Over time, using BPR on all major business processes allows you to spread these seven most important characteristics throughout your organization.

Conclusion

Why do all this? Because at the close of the 20th century—and well into the 21st—the individuals, organizations, and nations that thrive and prosper will share these characteristics and the resulting core competency. This competency, more valuable than any other, will be the ability to create change. Ultimately, this ability is the only competitive advantage that matters.

Americans and American organizations should not shy from the changes needed to maintain preeminence in world commerce and world affairs, and to solve the pressing domestic issues that impede our growth. We are, after all, a nation founded on radical change, by people who abandoned Old World ways to create a new world. We must recall that a little over 200 years ago *we the people of America redesigned the entire process of government, changing it from tyrannic despotism to the breakthrough called democracy.*

In the face of the challenges ahead, we should take heart that this pioneer spirit—courage, risk-taking, ingenuity, hard work, and the will to do what must be done—is at the core of our national character. Because this spirit is within us still, it will be, as in times past, our hope for the future.

Summary

- In the future, it will not be enough to carry out an occasional breakthrough project. Faced with a constantly changing competitive environment, your organization must develop a core competency of being able to create breakthroughs on demand.

- Within any organization it is possible to develop this core competency. A good way to start is by building the seven characteristics of a breakthrough organization into your next BPR project.

- It is time for all of us to remember that, without radical change, our nation would never have even been founded. We must once again draw on America's pioneer spirit for the courage to do what must be done for a future as glorious as our past.

APPENDIX A

BIBLIOGRAPHY

Allen, Brandt and Howard A. Downey, Jr., "The Conference Board 1991 Re-engineering Survey," The Conference Board, November 1991.

Bartholomew, Doug, "Vinyl victory," in "How You Fit in Re-engineering. . .and How You Don't," *Information Week* Supplement, May 5, 1992, pages 32-38.

Benjamin, Robert I. and Jon Blunt, "Critical IT issues: The Next Ten Years," *Sloan Management Review,* Summer 1992, pages 7-19.

Bowersox, Donald J., "The Strategic Benefits of Logistics Alliances," *Harvard Business Review,* July-August 1990, pages 36-45.

Boynton, Andrew C., Gerry C. Jacobs, and Robert W. Zmud, "Whose Responsibility Is IT Management?" *Sloan Management Review,* Summer 1992, pages 32-38.

Business Week, "Is It Time to Junk the Way You Use Computers?", July 22, 1991, pages 66-69.

Cameron, Kim S., Sarah J. Freeman, Aneil K. Mishra, "Best Practices in White-Collar Downsizing: Managing Contradictions," *Academy of Management Executive,* 1991, Vol. 5, No. 3.

Davenport, Thomas H. and James E. Short, "The New Industrial Engineering: Information Technology and Business Process Redesign," *Sloan Management Review,* Summer 1990, pages 11-27.

Dichter, Steven F., "The Organization of the '90s," *The McKinsey Quarterly,* #1, 1991, pages 145-155.

Eckerson, Wayne, "Firms Re-engineer Processes Via Information Technology: Most, But Not All, Redesign Efforts Pay Dividends," *Network World,* March 2, 1992, page 4.

Foster, Robert A., "Re-engineering the Lending Process," *Journal of Commercial Bank Lending,* September 1991, pages 48-51.

Gallupe, R. Brent et al., "Electronic Brainstorming and Group Size," *Academy of Management Journal,* June 1992, pages 350-369.

Gash, Debra C. and Wanda J. Orlikowski, "Changing Frames: Toward an Understanding of Information Technology and Organizational Change," paper submitted to the 1991 Academy of Management Meeting, Organizational Development and Change Division, January 1991.

Gould, Lawrence, "Advanced Technology Is Complex, But Manageable," *Managing Automation,* August 1991.

Gulden, Gary K. and Robert H. Reck, "Combining Quality and Re-engineering for Operational Superiority," *Perspectives on the Management of Information Technology,* September/October 1991.

Hall, Jim, "Integrating Technological Upgrades with Re-engineered Processes," *Industrial Engineering,* March 1992, page 16.

Hammer, Michael, "Re-engineering Work: Don't Automate, Obliterate," *Harvard Business Review,* July-August 1990, pages 104-112.

Heygate, Richard, "Memo to a CEO," *The McKinsey Quarterly,* #2, 1991, pages 44-55.

International Data Corporation, "Business Process Redesign 1991: The Confluence of Management and Information Technology Consulting," December 1991.

Jacob, Rahul, "Thriving in a Lame Economy," *Fortune,* October 5, 1992, pages 44-54.

Jacob, Rahul, "The Search for the Organization of Tomorrow," *Fortune,* May 18, 1992, pages 92-98.

Kaplan, Robert B. and Laura Murdock, "Core Process Redesign," *The McKinsey Quarterly,* #2, 1991, pages 27-43.

Knorr, Robert A., "Productivity: Business Process Redesign: Key to Competitiveness," *Journal of Business Strategy,* November/December 1991, pages 48-51.

Kotter, John P., "What Leaders Really Do," *Harvard Business Review,* May-June 1990, pages 103-111.

Krass, Peter, "A Delicate Balance," in "How You Fit in Re-engineering. . .and How You Don't," *Information Week* Supplement, May 5, 1992, pages 26-30.

Lee, Gary, "Workers Focus on Factory Flaws, Fixes: Discussion Groups Turn Up Discontent," *The Washington Post,* June 28, 1992, pages H1, H5.

Leibfried, Kathleen H.J. and C.J. McNair, *Benchmarking: A Tool for Continuous Improvement,* New York: HarperCollins, 1992.

Martin, James A., *Information Engineering: Book II — Planning and Analysis,* Englewood Cliffs, New Jersey: Prentice-Hall, 1990.

MIT Management, "Are Investments in Information Systems Paying Off? An Interview with Lester Thurow," Spring 1990, pages 14-16.

Prahalad, C.K., "The Changing Nature of World Competition: Reversing the United State's Decline," *Vital Speeches,* April 1, 1990, pages 354-357.

Ramelli, D.S. and Clifton Cooksey, "How to Run a Suggestion Program," *Incentive,* October 1991, pages 103-108, 218.

Moore, John, "Re-engineering Riddle," *Systems and Network Integration,* May 18, 1992, page 38.

Scott Morton, Michael S., *The Corporation of the 1990s: Information Technology and Organizational Transformation,* Oxford: Oxford University Press, 1991.

Sirkin, Harold and George Stalk, Jr., "Fix the Process, Not the Problem," *Harvard Business Review,* July-August 1990, pages 26-33.

Sheridan, John H., "Racing Against Time," *Industry Week,* June 17, 1991, pages 23-28.

Stalk, George Jr., "Time—the Next Source of Competitive Advantage," *Harvard Business Review,* July-August 1988, pages 41-51

Stalk, George Jr., Philip Evans, and Lawrence E. Shulman, "Competing on Capabilities: The New Rules of Corporate Strategy," *Harvard Business Review,* March-April 1992, pages 57-69.

Stewart, Thomas A., "U.S. Productivity: First But Fading," *Fortune,* October 19, 1992, pages 54-57.

Sugawara, Sandra, "Cutting the Paper Chase: Service Companies Find Computer Imaging Technology Boosts Productivity, Cuts Costs," *The*

Washington Post, August 17, 1992, pages 1, 18-19.

Walton, Sam, *Sam Walton, Made in America: My Story,* New York: Doubleday, 1992.

Whitney, Daniel E., "Manufacturing by Design," *Harvard Business Review,* July-August 1988, pages 83-91.

Wilkinson, Richard, "Re-engineering: Industrial Engineering in Action," *Industrial Engineering,* August 1991, pages 47-49.

APPENDIX B

BPR GLOSSARY OF TERMS

Activity Analysis
The analysis and measurement (in terms of time, cost, throughput) of distinct units of work that make up a function or process.

Breakpoint
The point at which the market—either the customer or investor—responds to a change in delivery of value in a way that yields the delivering organization a breakthrough economic gain.

Benchmarking
Comparing capability or performance of an activity, function, or process against an accepted norm. Involves identification of the factor to be measured, identification and surveying of appropriate sources of comparison, and sizing of the gap to be bridged. Often followed by the adoption of a "best practice" from the organization benchmarked.

Continuous Improvement
Constant incremental performance gain, usually implemented through an empowered workforce.

Culture
The basic assumptions and beliefs that are shared by members of an organization, that operate unconsciously, and define in a basic, "taken for granted" fashion an organization's view of itself and its environment. "Culture" includes the way people behave toward each other and the rituals and routines of organizational life.

Customer
Person or organization that receives the output of a process. Internal customers are people or processes within an organization who receive work-in-progress from other processes, then add further value to the work.

External customers are outside the organization and are the final recipients of output.

Flexible Factory
A production system that allows the quick rearrangement of how work is done in order to accommodate an ever-changing mix of outputs.

Just-in-Time
An approach to managing production that is designed to respond quickly to customer orders, and that minimizes in-progress and final inventory.

Methodology
Tool, technique, analytical, or delivery framework needed to provide a service.

Objective
The point aimed at; an expected outcome defined in a measurable way.

Organization
A system delineating the structure and reporting relationships between members. Organizing is the process of identifying and grouping work to be done, defining and delegating responsibility and authority, and establishing relationships to accomplish objectives.

Plan
A detailed and coordinated set of activities scheduled in order to translate a strategy into the actions deemed necessary and sufficient to realize its objectives.

Process
A set of logically related activities performed to achieve a defined business outcome. A process has the following components:

Inputs: Information and materials.

Throughput or transformation: People, supplies, methods, equipment, and environment.

Outputs: Goods and services produced, plus information about them or about process performance.

Business Process
A large process, usually made up of several smaller ones that are linked together to produce one or a family of similar outputs.

Core Process
A uniquely configured set of linked activities that specifically respond to external events (market forces, customers, suppliers, investors, government).

Process Improvement
Occurs when a component of a process is changed, and the change results in increased performance.

Process Simulation
Running trials of predefined models of the process to evaluate "what if" or "what could be" scenarios. (A number of computer tools and models can be used, such as SPARKS.)

Support Process
A process that is not central to creating value or to delivering competitive advantage, but which may be necessary for their viability.

Product or Service
What the customer buys.

Quality
The degree to which customers'/clients' expectations are satisfied.

Total Quality
A company-wide management philosophy that focuses on customer-supplier relationships, empowerment of staff, costs of quality, defects prevention, and so on.

Redesign or Re-engineering
Completely redesigning a process (as opposed to changing one or a few of its components) to achieve an identified new standard of performance.

APPENDIX C

ABOUT THE AUTHORS

Henry J. Johansson, CMA, is a Partner in Coopers & Lybrand's Manufacturing Consulting Practice in New York City. Specializing in the introduction of new technology to enhance performance and competitiveness, he is a board member of the National Coalition for Advanced Manufacturing and the Operations Management Association, and a member of the Conference Board committee dealing with technology and innovation. In 1988 he received the Outstanding Service Award from the National Research Council for his work on manufacturing technology. Mr. Johansson is a certified management consultant (CMA) in the Institute of Management Consultants and a certified practitioner in production and inventory management. His clients include Allied-Signal Corporation, Wal-Mart Corporation, AT&T, and Johnson & Johnson. On the board of advisors for the *Journal of Cost Management for the Manufacturing Industry,* he has published articles in periodicals such as *Leaders Magazine* and *Management Accounting.* He holds a B.S. degree from Manhattan College and an M.B.A. from Temple University.

David K. Carr is the Partner-in-Charge of Coopers & Lybrand's Center of Excellence for Total Quality Management in Washington, D.C., and the lead Partner in the firm's Change Management Practice. He leads a group of 75 consultants in providing clients with assistance in introducing new management systems, strategic planning, and operations improvement. Mr. Carr's 15 years' consulting experience includes work with Allied-Signal, Avea-Brown-Boveri, Dunlop Tire, McDonnell Douglas, the U.S. Navy, the Tennessee Valley Authority, New York Life Insurance, Saks Fifth Avenue, SEMATECH, and United Airlines. Before joining Coopers & Lybrand, Mr. Carr was an analyst with the Central Intelligence Agency. The co-author of the book *Excellence in Government: Total Quality Management in the 1990s* and a study of TQM in the federal government published in *Quality Progress,* he is a member of the American Society for Quality Control. He holds a bachelors and a masters degree in public administration from Pennsylvania State University.

Kevin S. Dougherty, in Coopers & Lybrand's Boston office, is the Partner-in-Charge of the Financial Services Resource Management Practice, which serves the banking, insurance, and investment company industries. He also heads Coopers & Lybrand's Financial Services Business Process Redesign Practice. His recent clients include the Bank of Boston, The Travelers, and Putnam Investments. Mr. Dougherty has been a keynote speaker for the Investment Company Institute Convention, the APIC Just-in-Time Convention, the Massachusetts Society of Public Accountants, and the International Business Communications/Mutual Fund Service Quality Conference. He holds a B.A. from Brooklyn College and an M.B.A. from Fordham University.

David E. Moran is a Partner in Coopers & Lybrand's Management Consulting Practice in Philadelphia, where he leads projects in business process redesign, organizational management, operational systems, cash management, product costing, and new service planning. He has over 20 years of consulting experience with clients in the commercial banking, insurance, health care, manufacturing, utilities, and services industries. A former president of the Method-Time-Measurement Association, he holds a B.S. in business administration from Loyola College.

Robert A. King, CMA, is a Partner in Coopers & Lybrand's Resource Management Practice in New York City. His 15 years of management consulting, with clients such as NYNEX, New York Telephone, Engelhard, Emerson, Knoll International, and Sandoz, includes work in process redesign, overhead value analysis, streamlining operating procedures, improving EDP support systems, work management techniques, and training in supervision. He has published in *The Journal of Business Strategy* and is the Secretary/Treasurer of the Institute of Management Consultants and an Active Arbitor of the American Arbitration Association. Mr. King holds a bachelors in business administration from Adelphi University.

INDEX

A

activity analysis   170, 172
activity-based costing   170, 172
Adler, Bill   69, 72, 183
ALCOA   18
Allied-Signal Corporation   6–7, 43–44, 60, 150, 152
anti-lock brakes (Bendix)   6-7
Apple   33
as-is structure   159–160
    analysis   170, 172
    performance and capability   172
    process mapping   169–172
AT&T   15, 124–125, 183
authority, delegation of   131
automation   14–16

B

Bank of Boston   4–6, 69, 112, 152
Bankers Trust   46
banks   46
Bear, Mike   35
Beavers. Alex   7
benchmarking   59–60
Bendix Automotive Services   6–7, 60, 150
Berberich, Lynn   102, 104
"best and brightest"   69, 72, 85
BF Goodrich, Geon Vinyl Division   58–59
bibliography   191–194
Blum, Mike   147
Boeing   96
brainstorming   172–173
breakpoint   37
    defining   150–154
breakthrough organization, creating   188
breakthroughs   1–21
    need   9
Burger King   28
business process redesign (BPR)   25–26
    principles   26–28
    TQM similarities and differences   133–134
    see also redesign

C

Cameron, Kim   115
Canon   33
capability

appraisal   60–63
as-is process   172
permanent BPR   83–84, 85
Carr, David K.   199
change
    lasting   143–144
    management   101–122, 160,
    162, 177
    potential   187–188
    structure   187
    sustaining   178
characteristics of breakthrough
organizations   182–189
Christ, Charles   35–36
Chrysler   14
Churchill, Winston   183
Ciba-Geigy   6
client-driven change   54–57
competition   8–14, 21
    competency-based   12–14
    parity   36–37
    sustainable advantage
    143–144
    time-based   12
    understanding   58
computer-aided design (CAD) 92
computer-aided manufacturing
    (CAM)   92
computers see information
technology
Congress, U.S.   19
Connecticut Mutual Life Insurance
24–26, 33
consultants   78–79, 82–83
    role   79–80
    selection   80, 81
Cooksey, Cliff   94–95, 118
cooperation, intra-organizational
120
cost effectiveness   146–147

creating breakthoughs   145–179
creativity
    fostering   142–143
    maximizing   156
    see also innovation
credit approval, improvement
program   37–38
cultural assessment   61–62, 109
culture change   117-120
customer demands   28–30, 57–58,
64, 183–184
    TQM   135–136
customer-oriented processes   29–31
customers   43–46, 130, 152 , 185
customer service   24–25

D

decision-making
    electronic systems for group
    96–97
    independent   120–121
design parameters   168–169
design team   160, 162
Discover phase   147–166, 179
    checklist   163–166
displacement   102, 112–114, 122
    planning for   162
dominance   182–183
Dougherty, Kevin S.   200
downsizing   17–18
    see also displacement; layoffs
Dun & Bradstreet   146–149, 154

E

economic impact of change 63, 64
Edison, Thomas 182
Eisenhower, Dwight D. 76–77
employees 186
    ideas 118, 132
entropy 126, 128
Ewers, Douglas 28–29
executives, role of 68-69, 75
Exxon 60

F

Farm Journal 6
feedback 131, 138–139
fiber optics 92
financial analysis, redesign
alternatives 173
financial officer, chief (CFO)
68–69
financial review 61, 62
financial services 15-16, 94-95
    see *also* Bank of Boston
flexible factory 5
Foster, Robert 15–16
Freeman, Sarah 115, 116
Frito-Lay Company 46
functional orientation 21

G

G2 Research Inc. 78, 80, 98
Gallupe, R. Brent 96–97
Gaye, Marvin 112
General Electric 54, 56
General Foods 48

General Motors 14–16
Geon Vinyl Division, BF Goodrich
58–59
glossary 195–197
goals 157–159, 182
    measurable 33, 35–36
Gordon, Bruce 58–59
greenfielding 27
Gretzky, Wayne 182–183
growth strategy 184–185
Gulden, Gary 28–29

H

Hardin, Joe 14
Hewlett Packard 57
human resources *see* staff

I

IBM 33, 113
implementation 77–78, 145–179
    planning 176–177
improvement, continuous 18, 26,
123–140
information
    management review 61, 63
    model 174–175
    systems redesign 93–94
information technology (IT) 46–47,
48, 87–100
    redesign 164, 166, 173
innovation 10, 38
    see also creativity
insurance company, redesign
42–43

see also Connecticut Mutual
inventory   13–14

J

Johansson, Henry J.   199
John Deere   6
just-in-time (JIT)   124–125

K

Kearns, David   60
King, Don   154
King, Robert A.   200
Kodak   48
Kotter, John P.   83

L

layoffs
        problems, practical   116–117
        psychology   115–116
        see also displacement
leadership   83, 162–163
        change   104–106
        IT and redesign   97–98
Leibfried, Kathleen   59–60
Limited, The   30–31

M

management
        planned change   77, 106–110
        planning   137
        role   47–48

management, total quality (TQM)
14, 25, 38–39, 124–125, 130
        BPR similarities and
differences   133–134
        commitment to   135
        elements of   135–140
        goals   136–137
        principles   126
Manning, Peter   4
manufacturing resource planning
system (MRP II)   88
mapping and modeling, redesign
alternatives   173
market   58–59
Martin, James   88–89
Means, Grady   57, 58
Medrad   44
Milliken Corporation   121
Mishra, Aneil   115, 116
Molenaar, Andrew   27
Moore, John   47
Moran, David E.   200

N

National Association of Suggestion
Systems   118
Naval Aviation Depot, Jacksonville,
FL   129–130, 132
Navy Public Works Center, Norfolk,
VA   114
New United Motors Manufacturing
Incorporated (NUMMI)   14
new ideas   183–184
new process, installing   177–178
North Carolina, state of   92
not-invented-here attitude   183–184

O

O'Neill, Paul 18
objectives *see* goals
Ojha, Helen 67, 68, 160
Olin, Len 15
operational review 61, 62
organizational assessment 61-62, 109
organizational culture, realigning 117–121
organizational framework 33, 34, 104, 105
outplacement 113
outsourcing 46, 114
Owens-Corning Fiberglass 44, 46

P

parallel development 167, 179
payback 36
performance 126,128–129
    as-is process 172
    assessment 157
    indicators 61, 63
Peters, Tom 33
Pfizer 6
pharmaceutical research 92, 93
PHH FleetAmerica 63, 69, 72, 75, 183
    change management 102–105, 113
    client-driven change 54–56, 57–58
    outsourcing 114
pilot testing, redesign alternatives 174
planners 76–77
planning change 145–179
Prahalad, C.K. 8–13, 33
Prebil, Jim 54, 55, 56, 57–58, 63
priorities 157
process mapping 169–172
processing modeling 95, 159-160
productivity assessment 16–18
project director 75–76
project management 162-163, 165
project manager 75, 85
psychology, staff who remain 115–116

Q

Qantas Airways 27–28
quality management
    (*see* management, total quality)
quality products 21
quick fixes 173
    long-term 140

R

Ramelli, Donnee 118
RayChem Corporation 12
readiness for change 104, 108
Realize results phase 175–179
    checklist 178
redesign 29–33, 42–43
    alternatives, testing 173–174
    ideas, generating 172–173
    processes 154, 157

TQM   134–135
   see also business process
   redesign
Redesign phase   166–175, 179
   checklist   175
resistance to change   110, 111
retail selling   93
rewards, employee   131, 139–140
Right Associates   18

S

shareholders   152, 185–186
Sirkin, Harold   29
skills   102
   see also staff, training
Society For Human Resources
Management   18
SPARKS   95–96, 160
staff   67–73, 85
   remainder after layoff
   115–117
   see also displacement
Stalk, George   29
standards   128
strategy   63–64, 66–67, 97–98,
149–150
structure, for change   187
super computers   92-93
suppliers   43–46, 186
systems re-engineering   80, 82, 97-
99

T

teams   67–73, 75–76, 102, 138
   building and training
   167–168

new   176
ownership and   130–131
redesign   166–167, 179
teamwork   118, 120
technical analysis, redesign
alternatives   173
temporary labor pools   114
textiles
   see *also* Allied Fibers,
   Milliken Corporation
time   73
Towers, John   5–6
Toyota   14
TQM   *see* management, total
quality
training   108
   team   167–168
   TQM   137–138

V–W–X
virtual reality   93
Viskovich, Fred   90, 96
Wal-Mart   13–14
Walgreen Drug   46–47
Walton, Sam   13–14
Wexner, Leslie   30–31
Wheeler, William   98–99
Whitney, Daniel   15
winning, obsessed with   182–183
workers, empowering   47–48
Xerox   33, 35–36, 60, 75, 84